Out of Nothing

Out of Nothing

A Cross-Shaped Approach
to Fresh Expressions

Andrew J. Dunlop

scm press

© Andrew J. Dunlop 2018

Published in 2018 by SCM Press
Editorial office
3rd Floor, Invicta House,
108–114 Golden Lane,
London EC1Y 0TG, UK
www.scmpress.co.uk

SCM Press is an imprint of Hymns Ancient & Modern Ltd
(a registered charity)

Hymns Ancient & Modern® is a registered trademark of
Hymns Ancient & Modern Ltd
13A Hellesdon Park Road, Norwich, Norfolk NR6 5DR, UK

Scripture quotations taken from the Holy Bible, New International
Version, Anglicised. Copyright © 1979, 1984, 2011 by Biblica
(formerly International Bible Society). Used by permission of
Hodder & Stoughton Ltd, a member of Hodder Headline Ltd.

British Library Cataloguing in Publication data

A catalogue record for this book is available
from the British Library

978 0 334 05668 3

Typeset by Manila Typesetting Company
Printed and bound by CPI Group (UK) Ltd

Contents

Acknowledgements

From the early days Berrywood Church was a collaborative effort. The vision was developed as a team, the ministries grew from the team, and relationships were built both within and through the team. To each person on the Core Team: thank you for being a part of the incredible journey that was Berrywood Church. I will continue to pray for you all as you grow in your faith and ministry. You are – in alphabetical order – Anna, Carol, Claire, James, John, Liz, Matt and Zara. (Your names have been changed from this point on!)

There were too many people in the wider Berrywood Church community and in the St Crispin's housing development to mention by name. We made such good friends. However, I do want to mention Jenny (not her real name, but she knows who she is!), to thank her for being willing to have her story told in some detail in Chapter 7 of this book.

Writing this book would not have happened without Pete Ward, who read my early thoughts on Jüngel and Root and encouraged me to write them up into a book. I would also like to thank David Shervington and the team at SCM Press for taking my proposal seriously and being willing to publish, and Nik and Michael for their comments.

Finally, I am indebted to my wonderful wife, Sarah, my partner in fun, work, ministry, parenting and a whole load of other things. Many of the events in this book would not have taken place without her – she played such an important role in the life of Berrywood Church. She also plays such an important role in my life! I am continually amazed at her ministry skills. She has had to suffer through reading drafts of this book, for which I am very grateful (even when she told me to change stuff).

Foreword

New Christian communities – what some call fresh expressions of church – are springing up in pubs, cafés and leisure centres, among people with a shared interest like classic cars, among groups with a similar outlook such as steampunks, in schools and workplaces, and in many other walks of life.

In this splendid book, Andrew draws out lessons from his own experience of helping to lead one of these communities. He also gives us much more. Through the lens of Jesus' crucifixion, he invites us to see these communities as opportunities for the church to respond to shadows of nothingness in the world around – the feeling that's left after a severe loss, after the destruction of a relationship or after the environment has been ravaged. Perhaps less acutely, a vague sense of emptiness, a feeling that there could be more to life, a longing for something better could be uncomfortable tastes of nothingness, milestones away from the fullness of life. What might it mean for a new Christian community to arise in response to nothingness?

If we follow the serving-first journey Andrew describes in Chapter 1 (see pages 15–16), a group of Christians listens to stories about nothingness in the local context. These may be stories with a subtext: 'We have nowhere to meet'; 'We have a shared interest but no opportunity to pursue it'; 'Life is a vacuum'; 'We don't have enough food'; 'We lack the skills to get a job'. As Andrew points out, these may be stories about a nothingness that's acutely felt, or about a nothingness that's real but scarcely noticed.

The group finds a simple form of loving and serving to fill the void. Often the loving service will be a gift that did not previously exist. A person who enjoys craft activities and someone else who enjoys telling stories may offer these as gifts within an all-age Messy Church, which fills several gaps: the initiative replaces the non-existence of friendships between families with an opportunity for families to get to know each other, while organizing crafts and telling Bible stories transform unfulfilled desires into loving service appreciated by others. Nothingness is countered with gifts.

As families keep coming back, community forms. 'Meetings' may be monthly but perhaps they also happen through WhatsApp and other contacts through the month. Informed by the values of the kingdom, the community will be one in which mutual giving is encouraged. At first there will be the giving and receiving of friendship. In due course these friendships will become a platform on which further gifts can be exchanged.

Perhaps someone arranges a rota for meals to be taken to a family whose mother is ill. Someone else gathers some friends to help a family decorate their new home. A third person is a regular source of wise advice. A fourth has an endless store of jokes. These gifts are reciprocated with expressions of appreciation, which affirm the giver and build the person's self-esteem. Not infrequently they give rise to return gifts of various types of kindness. Maybe experiencing this kindness alerts some people to its absence from their lives previously. They become aware of an earlier nothingness through their fuller experience of life.

These gift exchanges are scarcely reflected upon, let alone seen as building blocks of the body of Christ. But out of nothingness – the absence of desired friendship – a community emerges. And this community begins to have affinities with Paul's vision of the body characterized by mutual giving. For Paul, this giving took the form of spiritual gifts (e.g. 1 Cor. 12), supporting other Christian communities in need (e.g. 2 Cor. 8), and community members offering themselves (plural) to God and the world as a living sacrifice – singular; that is, acting as a unit (Rom. 12.1). Out of nothingness, the foundations of a *Christian* community are laid.

In time, for those who want, the community becomes a sense-making community. Some of the children sing songs from Messy Church at home. Families talk about some of the Bible stories they have heard. Maybe families at home are encouraged to read child-friendly versions of favourite Bible stories. Gradually, families absorb the Christian story, begin to make sense of life from within it and find that this meaning-making fills a hole in their lives. When they first came to Messy Church, exploring what it means to follow Jesus may have been far from most families' minds. Yet for some families, this increasingly becomes Messy Church's *raison d'être*.

Families begin to encounter God, often at points of nothingness in their lives – the emptiness of living alone perhaps, the loss of hope after a failed exam, the destruction of self-esteem brought about by bullying or the sense of helplessness in the face of impersonal and inflexible social institutions. As these encounters draw people towards Jesus, the community gradually evolves into an authentic expression of the church.

The fuller life believers experience sensitizes them to instances of nothingness among their friends and others outside the community. Led by the Spirit, they listen to stories that arise from nothingness, prayerfully look for simple forms of loving service that will fill the void, and repeat the journey they have experienced, but in their own way and in a manner appropriate to the context.

I find this understanding of fresh expressions provocatively helpful. It connects with the big theme of how God combats evil, which the tradition has largely understood as 'live' spelt backwards: evil is anything that tends to undo life. As such, all evil inclines towards nothingness, from physical destruction to actions that make the other person feel nothing inside. The mystery of the cross, as Andrew points out, is that Christ enters into nothingness in order to overcome it. His body is called to do the same, and new Christian communities are one outworking of this. Through the Spirit they enter the gloom of Good Friday and overcome darkness with Easter light.

Revd Dr Michael Moynagh
Wycliffe Hall, Oxford and Fresh Expressions

Introduction

'Throw your hat in the ring!' came the words from my training vicar as I told him about the job opportunity in another diocese: Pioneer Minister, Northampton West. I was coming to the end of my third year as a curate in a large city-centre evangelical church in Plymouth. This church, with its prominent location and civic responsibilities, had given me an excellent start to my ministry experience. There were four services on a Sunday, each with a distinct style. The congregation was active and engaged, we had lots of links into the community and there was a steady stream of people coming to faith through the regular Christianity Explored courses that the church ran.

But over the course of my curacy I began to develop an interest in fresh expressions of church,[1] aware that there were areas and groups of people in the parish we were barely impacting. In my final year, alongside a group of lay people and a Methodist colleague, we began to explore what a fresh expression might look like in the Barbican area of the city. This was a small area, one of the oldest parts of Plymouth, which had historically been a focus of activity through the fish market. After the market closed it became an area focused on creative arts, with quality bars and restaurants that drew tourists. There was plenty of new-age spirituality on show but little Christian presence. So we met regularly to pray over the course of several months in an artisan chocolate café and shop, owned by a Christian from another congregation who had a desire to use her business for God. This was exciting as the possibility of new things arose. We had a small team, a place to work from and the idea of starting a discussion group, initially based around the film *Chocolat*.[2]

Then I spotted the job advert by accident as I was browsing through the website of the Fresh Expressions organization. I went for it, not expecting to get it, but three months later I found myself moving into a house on a new-build development on the edge of Northampton, with my wife, Sarah, baby son and cat. The role was to pioneer new forms of church among people living in new-build housing developments on the western side of Northampton. I had long had a desire to serve in an area in which I could be at the heart of building community among the unchurched, as this is where I felt my personality and gifts lay. The idea of working on a new build was opened up to me by Revd Penny Joyce, whom I had met during my theological training when she was pioneering on a large development in Witney, Oxfordshire. Her example was an inspiration and opened up a desire that was confirmed to me while on retreat before my priesting in 2008. This job appeared to check all the boxes, so I was very excited to be moving in August 2010.

At that time Northampton was home to about 200,000 people and there had been extensive building around the edges since the 1960s. Now, with the Labour government focused on home-building, Northampton had once again been earmarked as an area for extensive growth. On the western edge lay the former village of Duston, which had been home to a large industrial component factory until 2002. This village was subsumed into the urban area of Northampton as it grew postwar, and further building in the 1960s, 1980s and 2000s took the residential population beyond the boundaries of the old village. On the edge of the village was a large estate that had belonged to the former St Crispin's psychiatric hospital, originally established as the Berrywood Asylum in the Victorian era. (The building was closed in 1995 and has lain derelict ever since.) These areas of development lay just three minutes' drive from the M1, from which London, Nottingham, Birmingham, Oxford, Cambridge and many other places could be reached in under an hour, making it an attractive location for commuters.

Northampton itself had good employment prospects, with some major banks and technology firms based on business parks on the outskirts of the town, and its central location making it an attractive base for warehousing and logistics.

Three areas in the pioneer role description were earmarked for thinking about. St Crispin's was the area we were living in, so this was the obvious one in which to begin. The new-build development sat in the grounds of the former hospital, dominated by the latter's derelict buildings. The intention was that these buildings would be converted into luxury apartments with underground parking, a community hall and plenty of outside space. When we arrived, only two of the old hospital blocks had been renovated, a situation that remained the same throughout my time there. The hospital's cricket ground and bowling green had been preserved and were now owned and used by local clubs. The derelict building was surrounded by white builders' hoarding and dominated the centre of the estate. Around the hospital were houses and flats built in a more recognizable new-build style, ranging from one- and two-bedroom apartments to five-bedroom detached houses. Also on the development was a large self-contained private retirement village (which was very difficult to get access to), a post box, a small play park for under-fives, and the local Church of England primary school, which had moved from Duston village to brand-new premises, doubling in size in the process. The first shops arrived several months after we did (but six years after the first residents moved in), and included a café, grocery store, beauty salon and toyshop. There were also plans for playing fields and a community centre with changing facilities. The café and toyshop would become important to our pioneering activities. Due to being situated in previous cultivated grounds, St Crispin's had something of a countryside feel to it. The large established trees that had been kept since the days of the hospital gave the development a settled feel, of having been around a lot longer than it actually had. The houses were relatively well spaced apart. There was an area of woodland in the centre of the estate and you didn't have to walk far to get to fields that were still being farmed.

The second area, separated from St Crispin's by one of the major roads into Northampton from the M1, was built in a completely different style. Upton, which had won awards for its design, contained a number of houses built in a very eco-friendly style. Although the range of the size of the houses was roughly the same as in St Crispin's, there was little space between them, and many were terraced. In front of each house there were fewer gardens; behind each block of housing was a large parking area. While Upton did have a community centre, opened around the time we arrived, other community facilities, such as a shop, were a long time coming. There was also a play park (suitable for over-fives), and an area of country park on the edge of the estate.

When we arrived, development in both St Crispin's and Upton had stalled due to financial pressures from the global recession, so although the road structures were in place, much of Upton in particular was open ground. The major road dividing the two estates meant that they were quite separate entities and did not operate as a single community.

In both estates there were high numbers of families with young children. Most of the kids were primary-school age and below, which meant that we, with our six-month-old baby, had some major things in common. Many were also educated to degree level and were pursuing careers in management or business. These were aspirational people building their lives, careers and families. Owning a new-build house, moving up the ladder, was part of that. Most of the homes were privately owned or privately rented. Upton had a higher proportion of housing-association homes due to the developers of St Crispin managing to satisfy the government quota for these by building the retirement village (though in fact this was very different from social housing).

The third area of investigation for fresh expressions was Sixfields leisure park. This was home to several leisure-based businesses, such as a cinema complex, ten-pin bowling centre and gym, as well as many chain restaurants. It is also the location of Sixfields Stadium, home to Northampton Town FC, to whom I would serve as chaplain for two memorable seasons.

In practice I began by focusing on St Crispin's, in part for pragmatic reasons: it is much easier to influence a community when you are resident in it. However, unknown to the diocese at the time of forming the job description, a Baptist pioneer minister had recently moved to live on the Upton development. It made sense, where we were doing similar things, to stick to the estate in which we were based, but we did manage to work together productively on a few projects during the course of my time there.

So these were the settings in which I was to pioneer. Even before arriving I had a loose idea of how I wanted to see the work develop. I expected anything that was created to be relationship-based and community-focused, with any activities arising from the relationships formed and the needs we were to encounter. Forming relationships in the community, something which fits my gifts and talents, was to be central.

This book will tell the story of pioneering in this setting, addressing the questions that arose during the process of developing Berrywood Church. The questions addressed in the first few chapters form the background for the overarching questions that shape this book: How might the validity, fruitfulness or success of a new ecclesial community be judged? What foundations or yardsticks are we to use? Pioneering ventures are often time-limited and have a specific set of outcomes or targets provided by the diocese or sponsoring organization. My project was no different. In this book I argue that not only can the notion of a cross-shaped church shape the form of church that develops, it can also inform questions of fruitfulness and success. This argument is played out in the final four chapters of the book.

Chapter 1 addresses some of the background to what I was doing in Northampton, engaging with some of the practical issues of starting out (such as building a team, naming a church and actively listening to the context), describing what we did at Berrywood. I also explore the development of the Fresh Expressions movement in the UK, which led to the writing of the influential *Mission-Shaped Church* report, which in turn fuelled the growth of contextual church-planting initiatives in the early twenty-first century. I offer some definitions of fresh expressions, unpacking what these mean for my context and describing the processes that are recommended in pioneering a new church.

In Chapter 2, noting that our fresh expression, like many others, attracted a fairly homogeneous group of people from similar backgrounds and in the same life-stage, I ask whether this is a legitimate place from which to start a new church. Can a church be homogeneous or should diversity be the aim? In doing so, I investigate the biblical basis for fresh expressions from descriptions of the early Church in the book of Acts.

Chapter 3 charts our progress towards creating a gathering for worship. From this experience I question what it is that makes a church 'church'. What elements or practices need to be present? In unpacking this question, I engage with different understandings of church from various traditions.

At Berrywood Church our starting point was to focus on building community on the new-build development. Chapter 4 describes what we did to this end, and I analyse the implicit theology behind our actions. I also engage with other writers on fresh expressions, asking what theological concepts have been used as a foundation for thinking about these new forms of church, including Trinity, *missio Dei*, the kingdom of God, and the Holy Spirt. For each, I ask whether these are the best theological bases on which to build an understanding of church.

Chapter 5 begins my argument that our understanding of the church should be cross-shaped. The church needs to be first and foremost about Christ, understood through the incarnation, life, death, resurrection, ascension and return of Jesus Christ. Using a broad concept of atonement, I analyse how different approaches to atonement affect the mission and shape of the church. I conclude that as God reaches out to the world (understood through atonement), so the church, as the body of Christ, undertakes Christ's atoning work in the world.

Building on this, I argue in Chapter 6 that the place of encounter with God is the best starting point to understand the work of the church in the world. God meets us, in Christ, out of nothing, at our places of nothingness; we bring nothing to the encounter. This place of encounter is a locus of atonement. I then suggest what God's atonement in this place of encounter might look like in the church, thus creating a cross-shaped church. From this vision, one then finds a theological foundation by which the effectiveness of a fresh expression of church can be measured.

In the final chapter, I come back to the question of what is success in the light of the previous discussion, re-examining some of my initial expectations about the size to which Berrywood Church might grow. Returning to the cross-shaped approach, I give concrete examples of how God was at work in the place of encounter through the initiatives of Berrywood Church and suggest that this should be the starting point for both shaping and evaluating new ecclesial communities.

Notes

1 In this book I follow the convention of using lower case when referring to an instance of a fresh expression of church, upper case when referring to the Fresh Expressions organization or movement.

2 Dir. Lasse Hallström (Miramax, 2000).

I

Where do we start?

The months of anticipation came to an end as the removal van pulled away, leaving behind a mountain of unpacking. We had arrived in our new house in the middle of the St Crispin's new-build development on the edge of Northampton. We were two adults, one baby and a cat, and we had a mandate to start church. We were eager to get going, throwing ourselves into building relationships with those who lived around us, but there were many questions buzzing around in our heads, the answers to many of them still unknown. What would our new church look like? Who would it be for? Would anyone actually join us? Where would we meet? What would we do when we gathered? How much of a vision should we set at the start? How will we get started? This was a blank sheet of paper, a fresh start for the Church in this community, so there were no set precedents or expectations. It struck me that the way to proceed was to take one step at a time, not getting too far ahead of ourselves. The first step was surely to build relationships with the people around us.

But before I discuss how we started and what we did, there is a more pressing question: Why are new forms of church needed? Surely the local parish church would be able to serve the needs of all the residents in their parish? In this chapter I will give a brief background to fresh expressions of church, define what they are and introduce some theory about how pioneering may take place. I then discuss the early questions we asked, the activities we began and the way we engaged with our neighbours.

What are fresh expressions and why are they needed?

From the middle of the last century there has been increasing recognition that some areas, cultures, subcultures or people-groups were not being reached by traditional forms of church. This can be seen through several factors. Official statistics show that attendance in Anglican churches in England and Wales has been in decline since the 1930s, with particularly steep decline in the last decade of the twentieth century, despite an overall increase in UK population in this time.[1] In 2001, the first year that there was a question about religion on the UK census, 71.8 per cent of British residents claimed affiliation to Christianity. This number dropped to 59.3 per cent by the time of the 2011 census. Clearly there are all kinds of reasons why someone may choose to answer this question in this way, from faith conviction to national identity, but the drop in numbers of those claiming Christian affiliation demonstrates an increasing reluctance to identify with the Christian heritage of the country. Also clear is that Christian affiliation alone does not translate into church attendance. Attendance across all denominations in Britain was estimated to be 5.8 per cent of the population in 2010, a number that has also been in decline in the last 40 years.[2] So both in terms of church attendance and Christian affiliation, Christianity appeared to be in decline.

Another factor is the changing demographic of traditional church congregations. Between 1979 and 2005, the number of churchgoers across all denominations who were over the age of 65 as a percentage of the total had nearly doubled, while that of those aged between 15 and 29 had shrunk by more than half (Archbishops' Council, 2007, p. 33). Bear in mind that this is half of a diminishing total and the full picture revealed by these statistics comes into place: congregations seem to be getting smaller and older. Anecdotal research reveals a similar picture. One can step into many churches across the country and see almost nobody between the ages of 12 and 40, and very few children. The implication is that these demographics are either not being reached by the local church or many people simply do not like what they find there.

This data needs to be read in context; it is simply not true to suggest that the Church has been universally in decline in the UK as Christendom has come to an end. There are numerous examples of new churches and growing churches that have been written about in detail. For example, David Goodhew, who heads the Centre for Church Growth Research in Durham, has written extensively on church growth and new churches established since 1980.[3] These are to be celebrated and we can learn from what they do well. Such growth is patchy across the country, and while some of it is within the historical denominations, growth can also be seen in free churches, new denominations and multi-ethnicity churches. In later writing focusing on the theology of church growth, Goodhew suggests that the 'theology of decline' implicit in Western Christian thinking needs to be discarded, not only because of the examples of growth that can be found but also because this theology can act as a self-fulfilling prophecy, discouraging some from investigating strategies and theologies that could lead to growth (Goodhew, 2015a, pp. 33–5). There are churchgoers who have worshipped for many years in the same church and have never seen it grow in their lifetime. The idea that the church inevitably shrinks can be difficult to shift, but this narrative must be challenged. Simply because a trend may be evident in the present does not mean it need always be so.

Sociological theories have also been built on the back of statistics of decline. For example, Steve Bruce, building on sociological contributions from the mid-twentieth century onwards, contends that as societies modernize, the desire for religious affiliation and practice reduces resulting in societies becoming more secularized. Secularization is an inevitable by-product of modernization. Bruce claims this secularization theory has been the driving force of the decline in religion in the West, and he sees no signs of this trend reversing (Bruce, 2002). This theory has rightly been challenged by, among others, Grace Davie, who sees the church maintaining an important role in people's lives even though they do not attend. They have a vicarious approach to the church, wanting it to be there, ready to be turned to should the need or desire arise (Davie, 2015, pp. 81ff.). This can often be seen in villages where the local church is earmarked for closure; the most vociferous opposition can come from those who hardly ever attend.

Despite this it is difficult to deny that attendance has been falling for many decades. Attributing it purely to secularization would be to accept that the narrative must always be one of decline. There are probably several factors that led to decline, none of which indicate that the trend must continue. Michael Moynagh, who has become an authority on new forms of church and whose work I will be exploring more fully later, mentions some of these factors. He writes that the development of (good) organizations and activities, in the latter half of the nineteenth century and first half of the twentieth, unintentionally acted in competition with the church (Moynagh, 2017, pp. 125–6). The welfare state reduced the role the church played in alleviating poverty, compulsory education reduced the role of Sunday schools, and an increase in organized leisure drew people to other places. At the same time, social pressure to attend church waned. Industrial owners who may at one time have insisted on or encouraged their workforce to attend church – such as Titus Salt or John Cadbury – were gradually followed by those with new attitudes. Overambitious church building, coupled with a reliance on philanthropy (neglecting teaching on regular giving), resulted in financial pressures once the number of philanthropists declined. This led to a focus on maintaining buildings, often having to cut ministry or outreach budgets to pay for them. Money raised went into maintaining the church rather than back out into the world. This can be described as a 'growing self-absorption', marking a slow withdrawal from the world and limiting imagination for new forms of church (Moynagh, 2017, p. 126). In short, the church failed to adapt.

Of course, if we were only interested in numbers, this would be concerning. Given that, with a missional interest, many in the church are passionate about helping others to connect with God, we do need to look at current practices and forms of church and ask whether they are serving their purpose. There are generations, cultures and subcultures in our country who were and are not being reached by traditional forms of church. In order to meet Jesus' call to 'make disciples of all nations' (Matt. 28.19), the Church needed a different approach to mission. Starting from the mid-twentieth century, it began to adapt, experimenting slowly at first.

Fresh expressions thinking developed from these early experimentations. As long ago as 1957, the Anglican bishop and missionary Stephen Neill, inspired by his experience in South India, recognized that traditional forms of church in the UK needed to change to meet the needs of current society. Speaking of larger cities where the church was on the fringes of the society and populations were becoming more mobile, he wrote:

> It has become increasingly recognized that it is useless to talk about bringing these people back to the Church. They have moved away from the Church, or perhaps have never been seriously conscious of its existence. It is for the Church to follow them, and to make their acquaintance in the places where they live and work. (Neill, 1957, p. 65)

He went on to talk about experiments in some British cities around small groups and celebrating the Eucharist in homes.

In a few places church leaders began to see the need to form new congregations in places that, for various reasons, were not being served by the parish church. This took the form of establishing daughter churches or church plants, which may or may not have met in ecclesial buildings. One example close to my new-build area of St Crispin's was St Francis Church. This was established in the wave of house-building in Duston in the 1960s. Several families moved from the parish church and were joined by new incomers. Some new church plants rented buildings and began to address cultural differences, reflected in the style and shape of church. The parish church in Chester-le-Street, County Durham, planted eight different congregations into different areas of the town between 1971 and 1984. They used the imagery of a strawberry plant sending out runners into new ground. Three of their church plants are still meeting today.

As a curate, my father planted a new congregation for families in a school on a council estate in Barking, East London, in 1972. After gaining permission to develop some simpler liturgy from the forward-thinking chairman of the liturgical commission, Ronald Jasper, they experimented with different forms of worship, including new technologies such as video clips, all informally delivered in jacket and clerical collar rather than robes. Since the intent was to communicate the faith simply and to grow disciples, they also ran their own sermon series rather than following the lectionary. About once a year he would preach a series on the Christian basics, but he also taught topically, on Christian attitudes to prayer, money or worship for example, and preached sequentially through some books of the Bible. To people from that estate, the location in a school hall formed less of a cultural barrier to access than the church building itself would have. This was all very innovative for the time – all this was taking place when the official liturgy of the Church of England was still the 1662 Prayer Book. He speaks of a congregation numbering from 60 to 100, made up mostly from young families living in nearby tower blocks who did not previously attend the parish worship. Although the PCC were largely supportive, there were the inevitable murmurings similar to those that often plague fresh expressions today, of whether the new venture would cost money and whether the families would ever come to 'proper church'. At some point after he moved on, this new congregation was moved into the church to join with the morning parish worship in a new family communion format, which apparently gave the existing congregation a real boost but may have marked the end of innovation and contextualization.

While this sort of planting was rare in the 1970s, it increased throughout the early 1980s but there was still no recognized strategy. This changed with the founding of the church planters network under the leadership of Bob and Mary Hopkins, and soon afterwards the first church-planting conference was held at Holy Trinity, Brompton (HTB) in 1987. The pace of church planting would increase throughout the 1990s as church planting caught on, aided by the 1994 Church of England report,

Breaking New Ground. Since then, HTB has pioneered the way in consistently releasing groups of people to revitalize closed or dying churches in London and, more recently, in other major cities.

The Church Army researcher George Lings has written a detailed account of this progression, so I won't repeat it here. However, he notes that around this time, church planters began to realize that there were groups of people who would not be reached with a geographical mindset to mission (Lings, 2012, p. 169). Charting an increase in the number of new church plants – 234 between 1990 and 1998 – he notes that some of those were targeted not at a geographical area but at specific groups of people (most frequently youth). As a result there was variation in styles of worship, depending on the cultural tastes of the intended congregation, and the new ventures met at different times of the week, not necessarily on Sundays.

The *Mission-Shaped Church* report of 2004 marked a further watershed in church planting. Recognizing that things had moved on in the ten years since *Breaking New Ground*, it offered examples of these new contextual forms of church that had been emerging over the previous decade, and introduced methodologies and a little theology. Wanting to avoid terms already in use, such as 'emerging' and 'emergent', which had been claimed by similar movements in the USA, the writing committee settled on 'fresh'. This reflected the promises made by new ministers in their ordination service to proclaim the faith 'afresh in every generation',[4] and effectively introduced the term 'fresh expressions of church' (Croft, 2008a, pp. 4–5). The report recognized that fresh expressions attempt to do something different from and more contextual than inherited church models, yet do not neglect the tradition of the church. Crucially, *Mission-Shaped Church* gave permission to parishes to try new things, and it rapidly became the springboard for the Fresh Expressions movement. Regardless of what label is being used, be it emerging, fresh expressions, new contextual churches or new ecclesial communities, *Mission-Shaped Church* offers an ongoing mandate. The support offered by the then Archbishop of Canterbury, Rowan Williams, helped move the language of mission and church planting away from its evangelical roots to be engaged with by those from all traditions. While there is still a long way to go before fresh expressions thinking is accepted by every part of the Church of England, the sheer range of traditions represented in the examples given on the Fresh Expressions website demonstrate that fresh expressions can work in charismatic, liberal, conservative and catholic traditions alike.

Definition

The Fresh Expressions organization defines fresh expressions as: 'new forms of church that emerge within contemporary culture and engage primarily with those who don't "go to church"'.[5] There are several key elements in this definition. First, they are a *form* of church. This indicates that the shape they take may look radically different from how church has usually been experienced. There is no pattern or blueprint that dictates how all fresh expressions will look, although different categories will have significant things in common, which will be discussed in Chapter 2. However, they are to be a form of *church*, therefore some of the marks of what it is to be church will be evident in the fresh expression. The answer to what these marks may be is not a straightforward one and different approaches will be discussed throughout this book.

Second, they are expected to 'emerge within contemporary culture', recognizing that working patterns, social interactions, life priorities have been in a rapid state of flux during postmodernity. Due to changing work and leisure patterns, Sunday mornings can no longer automatically be considered the best time to have a church service. When I was young (in the 1980s), there was little to do on a Sunday besides playing with friends or spending time with family. Now there are many choices of leisure and consumer activities, not to mention the increase in the number of people working in shifts. John Drane describes the current age as one in which – in the West – people are economically well off, with plenty of material possessions, yet more unsure of themselves, lacking confidence (Drane, 2008, pp. 2–28). Adulthood and its associate responsibilities are delayed as many enjoy an extended youth, taking opportunities to explore, find and define themselves. The social theorist Jacopo Bernardini rather harshly describes contemporary young adulthood as: 'tend[ing] to childishness without pleasure, to indolence without innocence, dresses without formality, has sex without reproducing, works without discipline, plays without spontaneity, buys without a purpose, and lives without responsibility, wisdom or humility' (Bernardini, 2014, p. 41).

Whether or not we accept Bernardini's analysis, without doubt society has changed dramatically from the days when inherited church traditions and practices were considered a foundation of British weekly life. The culture gap between church practices and general society has grown. Society is simply more fragmented and unpredictable. Making value judgements about it can be unhelpful. For churches to 'emerge [from] within contemporary culture', pioneers will need to understand and engage with the culture as it is in a particular place or with a specific group of people in order to speak gospel words of life into that culture. A certain amount of inhabiting the culture will be required before a relevant articulation of the gospel can be understood. Jonny Baker sums it up well:

> The challenge of mission is to go on an adventure of the imagination that enables mission to be done from the inside of the primal worldview and cultures. This leads to an articulation of the gospel that is local and indigenous rather than foreign and imposed. (Baker, 2015, p. 205)

Third, fresh expressions are to be established 'primarily with those who don't "go to church"'. They are not to be simply a cool new initiative for those who are dissatisfied with traditional church. Nor are they primarily to lure those who were previously members of a congregation back to church, although some of this may happen. They are intended to reach those who do not and have never had significant contact with traditional church, and who may never have been to a service beyond the occasional offices. Often these three categories of people are described as the churched, the unchurched and the dechurched, although recent discussion has added some nuance to these categories, recognizing that there is more complexity in people's backgrounds than they allow (Dalpra and Vivian, 2016, p. 26). The simple fact of mathematics is that as church attendance has declined over the last 20 years in the UK, the proportion of people who not only have never attended but whose parents also may never have attended is getting larger. There is no sense in which they can return to church as they never came in the first place. My understanding of the Gospels is that Jesus came to invite everybody to respond to living a life following him. If the message is to reach everyone, the church needs to find a way of reaching those subcultures and groups who are not being impacted by traditional parish churches – those people who may have no background in church or Christian faith. Fresh expressions of church are intended to grow organically from within a culture in order to be better suited to the people they are trying to reach.

Recent research by the Church Army into fresh expressions in three Anglican dioceses indicates that to a large extent they are doing what they intended. In 66 fresh expressions studied, the researchers Claire Dalpra and John Vivian found that 24 per cent of those attending were classified as unchurched in some way. Thirty-nine percent were found to be dechurched, 29 per cent churched and a further 8 per cent had grown up in the fresh expression (most likely a Messy Church or similar family-friendly congregation) (Dalpra and Vivian, 2016, p. 28). Although one might hope that the proportion of unchurched may be a little higher than a quarter, these statistics indicate that almost two-thirds of attendees were new to or returning to a church congregation. Therefore fresh expressions cannot be accused of transfer growth. Those who were part of another church before attending the fresh expression were often part of the sending team or attending another church congregation alongside the fresh expression.

The definition then goes on to talk about how they are formed:

[Fresh expressions] will come into being through principles of listening, service, incarnational mission and making disciples; it will have the potential to become a mature expression of church shaped by the gospel and the enduring marks of the church and for its cultural context.[6]

Listening, service and incarnational mission are seen as central to the development of fresh expressions to ensure they are suitably contextual. As they are to emerge from the culture, those who seek to establish fresh expressions immerse themselves within that culture, getting alongside people, discerning the rhythms and needs of the community, perhaps serving them in some way. Because of this, fresh expressions of church usually do not begin by establishing a worship service, however contemporary its style may be. There is an important place for this more traditional approach to church planting in the British ecclesial landscape, as the last 40 years have shown, typified by the regeneration of many dying or closed parishes in major cities through church planting initiatives such as those led by HTB. Recent research has shown that this type of church plant can reinvigorate local congregations, boosting the number of worshippers up to tenfold with no detrimental effect on surrounding parishes (Thorlby, 2016). However, there remain cultural groups that even these plants cannot reach or are not suited to, and geographical areas where a plant of this type may not be the most effective strategy to reach out in mission. Using the fresh expression approach, the pioneering team are able to tailor what emerges to that community by fully immersing in the culture, to some extent freeing them from preconceived ideas of what church should look like. Arising from deep listening, they tend to operate on an incarnational rather than attractional missional model. Fresh expressions begin where the people are, rather than encouraging them to come to a place where the church may set up. Fresh expressions are fully contextual.

The listening-first approach raises difficult questions. It is difficult – and inadvisable – to come in with a preconceived plan, therefore much time for discernment is needed. The perception may be that the pioneering team initially spends plenty of time apparently doing nothing, as they 'hang around' in a godly way. But in this time they are intentionally making connections and building relationships in that culture. This can raise issues with the sponsoring organization, church or diocese, who could be impatient to see results. Taking such a contextual approach may also raise the question of whether what emerges can legitimately be called church. Fresh expressions have developed in a huge variety of ways, which can look quite different from traditional church.

The definition above also recognizes that fresh expressions do not have to look like church straight away. They have the 'potential to become a mature expression of church'. This statement clearly needs unpacking, and the marks of a 'mature expression of church' will be explored throughout the book, although discipleship, also mentioned in the above definition, should be one of those marks. However, the 'intention to become church', whatever that may look like, should be embedded within the aims of the project. An activity that has no intention to form a church community or congregation may simply remain a piece of missional or social outreach. There may be value in it, but it cannot be called a fresh expression of church.

Michael Moynagh, in his comprehensive book, *Church for Every Context*, introduces theology and methodology for fresh expressions and church planting, developing it in his follow-up *Church in Life*. He initially refers to such initiatives as 'new contextual churches' (2012, pp. x–xiii), freeing them up from the language of fresh expressions often associated with the Anglican and Methodist churches, but later revises the description to 'new ecclesial communities' (2017, p. 4). He identifies four qualities of such communities, which echo those set out in the fresh expressions definition above. They are to be missional, intended for people who do not usually attend church; contextual, appropriate for the culture they seek to serve; formational, with an aim to make disciples; and ecclesial. He writes: 'The intention to become church marks out new contextual churches from mission initiatives or projects. The aim is not for the initiative to be a stepping stone to existing church but to encourage church to emerge within it' (Moynagh, 2012, p. xiv).

His later definition of 'new ecclesial communities' leaves open the question of whether they can currently be described as proper church (an ongoing question for many fresh expressions), while focusing the language on the communities themselves – the relationships that exist between people in the venture rather than the forms or structures of the 'church'.

In my context, taking a fresh expressions approach to mission in these new-build areas appeared to be the best way to begin. The local parish church and daughter church served a population of 20,000, which was growing due to the scale of development in the area. Their team rector had departed two years earlier without being replaced, and this was unlikely to change in the short term. This left the large parish being led by a full-time team vicar and a part-time non-stipendiary minister. Two years before he left, the team rector had moved on to the St Crispin's development as one of the first inhabitants, and had been involved in discussions around planning before that. He had initiated an ecumenical programme of welcoming, knocking on doors of new residents as they arrived and presenting them with local information about the churches and local facilities. This continued throughout my time in other developments around the parish. There was also ecumenical engagement with a small group of Christians in the retirement village. Beyond this, on the departure of the team rector the remaining team did not have the time or energy to engage with the incoming residents of the new build in a meaningful way, apart from offering baptisms, weddings and funerals. The congregations themselves were relatively small and did not have much of an understanding of mission. Reaching out or planting from these congregations would have been difficult at best.

A further constraint the parish church faced was in the way the developments were laid out. St Crispin's was built as a community with its own centre. The residents would naturally not have much affiliation with the old village of Duston, where the parish church was based. This applied even more to the

Upton development, separated from the village by major roads going into Northampton or out to the motorways. Residents of these developments would more naturally look towards Sixfields retail and leisure park for their day-to-day needs, and towards Northampton town centre or Milton Keynes, only 25 minutes away, for more major requirements. They would hardly have the need to head towards Duston. So the diocese made the decision to employ me as a pioneer, free from parish responsibility, to dedicate myself to these areas and build up a congregation organically around the more transient professional people who lived there.

Where do I start?

I had been given a line manager, a steering group and a mentor to support me through the project. The line manager was Charlie Nobbs, who had led a small team to plant a church in the large new-build development of Grange Park, situated to the south between Northampton and a major junction of the M1, about six miles from St Crispin's. He and his wife had been there for nine years when I arrived. By then, Grange Park Church was a major focus for the community as they offered important support groups for the large number of parents on the development, engaged in children's work, and had opened the only café in the area, which was proving popular. Their Sunday congregation had grown from the planting team of around 10 to nearly 100, many of whom lived on the estate. My line manager was to be my key person for guidance and accountability in my new role. The mentor had been pioneering elsewhere in the diocese in the new-build village of Mawsley for the three years of his curacy, and was now the Anglican minister in an ecumenical church in a nearby village, which was also growing due to home-building. The steering group was made up of my line manager and key stakeholders from the diocese. There was initially funding for five years, providing us with a house on the estate, a stipend and a budget of £5,000 per year to cover start-up costs until we could be financially self-sustainable. I would have to report to the steering group every 6 to 12 months throughout the project, part of which would be developing a plan for the new venture after the end of the five-year period.

Because the post had grown out of a desire to start something new, the writing of my job description had been influenced by fresh expressions thinking. This allowed me to start with a blank sheet of paper and also, helpfully, did not specify the shape the fresh expression should take, allowing the project to emerge from contextual thinking. It did, however, recommend a process for pioneering in the form of project milestones, which have since been written up for the benefit of other dioceses (Withington, 2011). These were useful as they allowed the fresh expression to develop and be assessed without focusing on numbers or form. The first milestone covers the first six months of the project: 'The pioneer would be asked to spend the first 0–6 months mapping the community and network possibilities within their area.' After this (milestone 2), the next 18 months were to be spent developing initial contacts, 'grow[ing] in engagement from 6–24 months with these networks with the view of starting appropriate mission work in the new build area'. The final two milestones spoke about the emergence of a Christian community and developing sustainability. These milestones echo the process for pioneering that the Fresh Expressions organization and others recommend, which recognizes that the development of Christian community emerges from listening and serving activities. This is known as the fresh expressions journey or the serving-first journey (see Figure 1) (Moynagh, 2017, p. 45).[7]

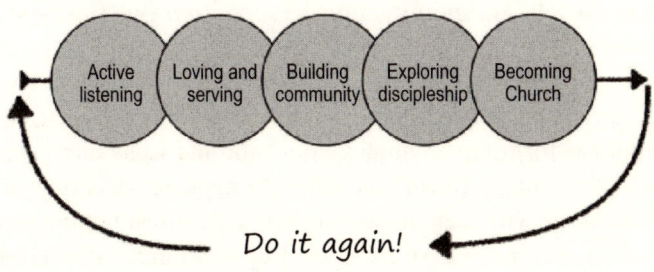

Figure 1: The serving-first journey

The milestones were helpful not only because they provided a map for engagement but because they had the initial six months built into them in which nothing tangible was expected, allowing the project to unfold at a sensible pace after sufficient background work had been done. The diocese had also made it clear that I was not to help out at the local parish church, as the temptation would be to get sucked into churchy things instead of being engaged in my community. This time was for intentional relationship-building, for getting involved with the community, for mapping the resources and groups that were there, and for ascertaining the needs or potential ways in. During this time I would continually ask what God is doing in the area, and what church might look like for these people.

My first challenge was how to introduce myself in a way that my new community would understand. It was when the British Telecom man came around on our second morning to connect our line that I realized my job title of 'Pioneer Minister, Northampton West' would be meaningless to most of the population. Before then I had mostly had to explain my role to Christians from my previous church, who were familiar with the language of mission and fresh expressions. I realized during this conversation that I would have to find different ways of expressing myself in explaining my role. I had already decided that the phrase 'Community Minister' would make more sense to the unchurched than 'Pioneer Minister', but it would still need some unpacking in the initial stages, given I had no church or congregation. Similarly, the language of 'fresh expressions' would just sound like jargon to those not in the know. I came up with a few different options:

I'm the new community minister, here to try to form a new church.

The drawback with this was the word 'church'. I wondered if the phrase 'form a new church' would automatically turn people off, as they might already have a stereotype of what church is (and reasons why they did not already go!). I also wondered if, in saying that, people would steer clear, as I might be perceived as a vicar on the lookout for recruits. Another attempt:

I'm the new community minister, here to help the church engage with the community better in this area.

This is better, but the question that might naturally follow is: 'Which church do you work for?' The answer was, of course, no specific church but for the diocese in general. It might lead the conversation down the wrong track and not give a clear idea of my role.

I'm the new community minister, here to support the community in whatever ways are needed.

Initially this was more accurate and was the approach I chose. My starting brief was to get to know people and find ways to support them. Forming church was some way down the tracks. From this starting point the conversation might lead to how I might support the community, and then we could start talking about residents' groups, toddler groups and other needs, seeing where it all might lead.

The next step was to get involved in the community. We started making the most of natural gatherings that were open to us. Our son was still a baby, so school-gate conversations weren't ones we could easily enter into; but we could spend plenty of time hanging out at the local park and being intentional about chatting with other parents. We quickly discovered that people were usually quite happy to chat after the ice had been broken. I also joined the newly formed residents' association. Shortly before we arrived the developers announced intentions to build new housing that was not in the original plans. This was to be developed before much-needed community facilities that had been promised. A residents' association was formed in reaction to this, initially to place some political pressure on the developers. Although the impetus was practical, those who joined quickly decided to invest some energy in forming community too. This move was a huge boost for me, as it meant I could join such a group without having the administrative challenges of starting it, and I could join it right at its inception when people were still open to meeting one another, collaborating and coming up with ideas. To start with I joined the meetings and introduced myself, and listened. A few weeks after we arrived, the group organized a morning to clear a section of footpath that had become overgrown and impassable. The path was supposed to be looked after by the developer but they had shown little interest in doing so. It led to a good time of making connections with the 20 people who came out to help. The path was cleared in about two hours but in going there, I had made a connection with a father in his thirties who would become central in getting one of our community groups up and running. I soon volunteered to sit on the subcommittee responsible for social gatherings, and later on a group discussing the details of the proposed community centre.

The social subcommittee had been busy organizing their first events too. The first was a Big Picnic on a late summer afternoon, with games for adults and children, a face painter and a piñata donkey for the kids. Over a hundred members of the community came out. For me it was a valuable time of getting to know more faces on the estate and listening to people's stories. Although I had met people on the residents' association, I hadn't met their partners or children. It was good to get my face known a bit too and introduce myself as the Community Minister. My wife had the bright idea of baking a large number of chocolate-chip cookies and going around sharing them with people, thus making introductions easier. It worked, and led to some great initial conversations. Soon a larger evening event was planned, with live band, fireworks and a hog roast to celebrate St Crispin's day. After such success, the subcommittee were making firm plans to do something at Christmas. All along I was using these opportunities to listen to people and discern what God might be calling me to do first.

Building a team

'If you don't have a team of people with you, then your ideas will struggle to blossom. If you have the wrong people with you, again your ideas will struggle to blossom' (Male, 2016, p. 24). While my wife and I were getting stuck into the community, being intentional about getting to know people, we were conscious that we needed more than just the two of us to make a real difference. The right people could help develop and share the vision, take responsibility for various aspects of the pioneering venture, and we could begin to form a pattern for Christian community together. So we started intentionally looking for other Christians to join us. The first came quite naturally. We had been out for a walk around the development one Sunday afternoon when we got talking to one of our neighbours, Kate, the mother of a ten-month-old boy, who lived down the street with her husband, Charlie. In conversation we found out that she was a fringe member at a town-centre church but often struggled to get to church. Until recently she had been in a prayer partnership with the curate from that church who had just departed to another post, and she missed that relationship. We invited Kate and Charlie around for dinner and became friends. Shortly afterwards she began to meet with my wife during the day to chat, read the Bible and pray. As we got to know her better and she started to understand what we were trying to do, she was keen to be a part of a core team that would think and pray through things. At around the same time the vicar of that town-centre congregation invited me to come and speak. They had a history of planting or supporting new congregations – Grange Park Church had been planted from there – and they were eager to support me too. I was overjoyed to hear the vicar say I could come and present what we were hoping to do, and if anyone wanted to join with us, that was fine by him. He had no worries about losing people to missional ventures. From that opportunity, one young couple who lived in a neighbouring village to St Crispin's began to explore what being part of our pioneering project might be like for them. A few months later this couple also joined our core team. A year later I was invited back to present again, explaining how the vision had developed during that time and what we had been up to. Again, one more contact was made with a young man, Michael, who lived near the development and became quite important to some of the ministries we were to run.

A final core team member also came to us through a neighbourhood encounter. We had seen the young professional couple who lived in the house right opposite us coming and going to work each morning for several months, but we had never had the opportunity to introduce ourselves properly. However, it was clear that she was pregnant, and the bump was slowly getting larger. Sarah and I decided that as soon as we noticed that the baby had arrived, we would pop over with a bunch of flowers and introduce ourselves. They welcomed us in and we got chatting. It turned out that Helen, the new mother, was a practising Catholic who struggled to get to church on a Sunday but gained a lot from going to an annual camp with worship, community and Bible-teaching. Shortly Helen joined Sarah and Kate in meeting to pray together while their children played. This was to become our first regular ministry. Helen's husband was not a practising Christian but was a lovely bloke with whom we also became friends and who joined us for quite a few of our events. We became good friends with them. A year later we were joined by Helen's twin sister, Tina, who had moved back into the area and eventually also joined the core team.

One other couple – residents on the development with whom I had made contact through a similar opportunity in a different church – started exploring the possibility of joining us too. After journeying with us for a few months they decided this wasn't the right place for them, a decision hastened by my phrasing something to them poorly. This left me disappointed, and annoyed at myself. The core team getting smaller was not something I'd hoped for! At the time I was discouraged, as it felt as though the church was shrinking before it had begun, but in hindsight I can see that this was exactly the right thing. Even without my poor choice of words, I expect they would have left before long anyway, as our ideas did not match their expectations. At the beginning of a project it is important that all those involved are united in their purpose, willing to commit to the group and move forward in their thinking together. It became clear that this couple wanted to belong to a church rather than shape it from the beginning, so we went our separate ways.

The new core team began meeting together about six months after we'd arrived in Northampton, fitting neatly with the milestones I'd been given. Initially we brainstormed the values we wanted to shape our new community, read the Bible and prayed together, and began exploring some of the fresh expressions theory. Several months later we booked a farmhouse in the Derbyshire dales for a time of bonding and vision-casting, which gave us a more focused time of thinking together and cemented us in our friendship.

What should we be called?

Having decided how I should introduce myself, as Community Minister, once we started doing things in the community it was important to have a name for the group. Writing about setting up a fresh expression community out of Gloucester Cathedral, Michael Volland warns against rushing into deciding on a name too quickly, as it could create preconceptions in people's minds about what you are or what you are not (Volland, 2009, p. 104). At the beginning of our pioneering, a name was not too important, as we were focusing on relationships. We found that once people got to know who we are, they started associating certain activities with us anyway, regardless of the lack of name, thus avoiding any negative preconceptions that might come with an ill-considered one. On the other hand, as soon as there were activities that we wanted to advertise beyond word of mouth, we thought a name would be important so that people knew who was behind them. We did not rush into this decision, eventually deciding on the name 15 months after we arrived in Northampton.

The advantage of being part of a denomination such as the Church of England is that it lends a sense of permanence and continuity to individual churches. People recognize the brand and tend to trust what they are doing, whether or not they find it interesting or relevant. Anything we do would have the Church of England logo on it, but we also needed a name to describe who we were more locally. However, if a name is poorly chosen, it may not attract or make sense to the people that you are trying to reach, or might exacerbate negative pre-conceptions that people may have.

A good church name should communicate something of the vision and values of the church but should also make it clear that it is in fact a church community, as opposed to some other type of group. As we were hoping – at this point – to become a church with a network of different outward-looking activities, relevant and open to everyone, the name should not be from a bygone era. Anything too clever would be also be a mistake and would probably date fast.

Some churches with a network vision, such as those in London, West Bromwich, Essex and Exeter, simply brand themselves as '[Location] Network Church'. The church in St Albans was at the time simply called 'Network!', which I felt didn't communicate anything understandable to the outsider. Other churches have dispensed with the word 'network' and picked a name based on location or on a Christian principle or metaphor. There is a danger, if the name is too cool, that it won't be seen to be a church or will quickly date. The Carpenters Arms in Sandwich and Deal, Kent, has advantages. To the non-Christian it might sound like a pub, yet it also refers clearly to Jesus and even to the cross. However, it can be a little difficult to find on Google, which comes up with a list of pubs.

Dave Male, the current National Adviser for Pioneer Development for the Church of England, planted The Net Church in Huddersfield in the early 2000s. In his book, *Church Unplugged* (2008, p. 22), he claims that the most important aspect of choosing a name was that the team came to the decision together. The process was more important than the destination. The Net was not his suggestion, but he came to like it and never regretted the decision. It is not such a bad name as it indicates the network church that it is, as well as drawing on the image of Jesus calling his disciples to be fishers of men.

I felt it important that our name should have the word 'church' in it, so as not to cause confusion about what sort of group we were. We also wanted to avoid the name 'St Crispin's', which might have been the obvious choice given the development on which we were based, but because there were so many other organizations in the immediate area that used that name (the retirement village, the former hospital, the cricket club, the bowling club, the nearby social club, the local men's tailors and the newly opened chippy), it seemed best to go for something else. We picked Berrywood Church, as it was clear who we were – a church – and gave an indication of our location. We were based on the St Crispin's development, at the centre of which is a small woodland called Berrywood. (There were also roads nearby called Berrywood Road and Berrywood Drive, and parts of the former hospital used to be called the Berrywood Asylum.) Another helpful factor was that there isn't another church in the world with the same name, so the domain name was available and a Google search would instantly bring us up on the front page.

Active listening

In order to understand a context fully, especially given that we had arrived from outside the area, it is important to get to know the people, the places and the rhythms of life in the area. This is why the serving-first journey begins with active listening. Before going in with a plan, the pioneer must spend time discerning what the priorities of the people are. What are their motivations? What are their needs? What values do they live by? How do they like to spend their time? A lot of our listening was informal. We threw ourselves into building relationships, inviting people around and hearing their stories. Through the residents' association meetings I was able to hear their concerns and desires for the community. We were out walking the streets regularly, visiting the play park and chatting with those we met. I also wasn't afraid just to hang around, either in the coffee shop or with neighbours. One neighbour who worked shifts occasionally got bored during the day when his wife was at work and his child was at school. After doing his chores (his wife would leave a list!), he would spend some of the day playing on his Xbox. I do remember spending a few afternoons joining him in that. On other occasions I made a point of spending time among the newly opened businesses. I would regularly go just to hang out in the café or chat to the owners of the men's tailoring shop or the independent toyshop. The toyshop owner was a retired teacher who had started the business in order to give herself a focus in her retirement. She was very intentional about welcoming children and families in after school, laying out things for them to do. This relationship-building was not wasted. When the residents' association eventually became less effective in community-building (due to poor leadership), the café and toyshop owners were ready to step into the gap, and we ended up doing several events together.

One of the first groups I attempted to organize was a weekly informal five-a-side football group. This was partly for my own reasons and partly to help build community. I had been used to playing a game of informal football each week for the last ten years, first in Oxford and then in Plymouth. On moving to Northampton I missed this, but saw it as a potential opportunity to build some relationships. Pioneering can come from our own passions and interests when aligned with the needs of the community. Through the residents' association I identified one person who wanted to join (the neighbour who played Xbox), and through a neighbourhood contact met another who was keen. They put out feelers with other dads at the school gate and through work contacts. Although for the first week I had to call in my cousin from a nearby town and a neighbouring curate to make up the ten, our numbers quickly grew and we always had enough for at least five-a-side. Monday Night Football was born. The fact that it was informal proved to be one of the attractive points. Most of us were dads who wanted a kick-around but had no desire to arrive home with a broken ankle because things were too competitive. I was also keen to instil from the beginning that this was a community activity, so we made a point of going to the pub each week after our game. Not everyone came, as some preferred to rush straight home again, but during the first couple of years we usually had a good number. Conversations covered all things, and on many occasions became quite serious about matters of faith.

With these relationships in place I was ready to do some more intentional listening. I wanted to know what non-churchgoers actually thought about church, and I hoped this information might shape the way we did things. An excellent Indian restaurant had just opened on the development, so I selected three people to take part in what I called a 'market-research evening' on the subject. They knew what my role was and we all got along well. They all agreed to come, bribed by the prospect that a hefty contribution to the beer and curry was coming out of my budget!

The purpose of the evening was simply to get the opinions about church from a group of men who do not normally or currently go to church. I had a number of questions lined up, and the conversation flowed as well as the beer and curry. All of them were in their mid-thirties, married or recently separated. Two were dads, while the third was expecting his first child in a few months. Two of the men had some church connection in their childhood, one being involved in a Boys Brigade, while another was taken to church until the age of about 12, at which point his parents stopped going. The only experience of church the third person had was of baptisms, weddings and funerals.

I asked about their first thoughts or impressions when they heard the word 'church'. Speaking of experience from a baptism, one remarked that it was too long, irrelevant, and most of it wasn't explained. The impression was that churches were full of old people. Having said that, all of them had been to services they enjoyed. Typically these were when the vicar or leader had involved the young people and the service had been more informal. One had been to a baptism at the town-centre church in Northampton and had enjoyed it due to the informality of the service and the contemporary music. They all agreed that church is boring if it doesn't relate to real life.

Regarding God, all believed in some sort of higher power or a power outside of themselves. One person mentioned the word 'fate' and the other two disagreed, saying life is pointless if it's all fate.

What about Jesus? They said he '100 per cent existed'. They knew about the cross, but preferred the idea of Jesus as a storyteller who spreads the word.

After that discussion, which went off at several interesting tangents, I asked the question: 'What would your mates at work say if you told them you were going to church every week'? They responded: 'They would take the piss.' A story was shared of a female colleague who went to church to get her child baptized but became a regular afterwards because she liked it and wanted to take the baptismal promises seriously. Some of her friends gently mocked: 'She's got religion!'

But what about negative stereotypes of church? One of the men responded that these, coupled with a bad experience at a christening he attended, put him off a little, confirming his pre-conception that church is boring and irrelevant. Another said that nothing had put him off in particular, but church 'has to be a family thing' that you are brought up into, and it is unfortunate that the tradition of the church hasn't changed with the times. The third member of our discussion said that because his family got out of the habit of going, so too did he. As he grew up it moved down the pecking order of what is important. With more work pressures, family commitments and other external pressures in a materialistic society, there appears to be less time to do church. This flowed into a discussion on contentment. All agreed that it is better to be content with what you have rather than constantly chase the next thing, as this will not lead to happiness. I mentioned that contentment is spoken about in the Bible (Phil. 4.11–13).

Next we talked about what church should be like. What did they think should happen in church? They replied that it should be informative and relevant – linked to the issues of the day. There should be plenty of interaction and involvement from the congregation so it isn't all upfront; the congregation should be participants not just observers. Church should be culturally relevant but not too extreme. Church should also give a sense of 'being wowed' to those who come. There should be some mystery, colour and excitement. But everything that happens needs to be explained; one cannot assume that people automatically know what's going on. One of the group, after mentioning his experiences of visiting places of worship in other cultures while on holiday, articulated the element of mystery beautifully, saying: 'Everyone else's religion seems to be more colourful and exciting, whereas we get a chocolate egg in a wet garden.' I found this extremely interesting and made a note to think more about the place of mystery and creativity in worship.

Finally we spoke about convenient times for holding a service. I was already aware that church now had to compete for attention with many other activities on a Sunday morning, so I asked them without pressurizing them: 'If you were to come, when would be the most convenient time for a service?' The first time mentioned was Sunday morning, 'because it's tradition', but that was quickly passed over. It was also said that Sunday lunch is also a tradition, and 'It's difficult to get lunch in the oven and ready when you're at church in the morning.' They concluded that timing of a church service has to be convenient for the whole family. There is too much going on on a Saturday, and they wanted to keep Sunday morning free for children's sport. Weekday evenings were busy, as often one or both parents worked late, then had to get home, make dinner and make sure the kids' homework was done. So they settled on Sunday afternoon, in the 3–4 p.m. slot, 'after lunch'. I'd had a hunch Sunday afternoons might be the best time, so it was great to have that confirmed.

All in all it was a very good evening and gave lots of things to think about. Many of their answers simply confirmed a lot of recent thinking about church, such as the need to be clear, relevant, inclusive, participatory and contemporary. More importantly for the men present, I could tell they enjoyed it and might be keen to do it again. I broached the subject of getting together every few weeks over a meal, using the Table Talk for Blokes[8] material to stimulate conversation. They were excited to do this, so 'Curry and Questions' became a regular six-weekly appointment. Initially we confined it to these three men, before opening it up to others after a year or so. It seems that a group of people sharing a meal together and talking about life and faith is an attractive thing to do!

We had a name and a core team and were becoming a close community of our own. We had built up good relationships in the wider community and had discerned a direction. We'd engaged in listening to the residents of the development (something that would be ongoing), and as a result had started some community activities and joined in with some already going on. This set the stage for what was to come but also began to raise questions, which will be addressed in the remainder of the book.

Notes

1 For more detailed analysis, see the *British Religion in Numbers* database of religious research: www.brin.ac.uk/figures/church-attendance-in-britain-1980-2015; accessed 26 May 2017.

2 'Church Attendance in Britain 1980–2015', *British Religion in Numbers*: www.brin.ac.uk/figures/church-attendance-in-britain-1980-2015; accessed 3 Oct. 2017. Also see Brierley (2008, pp. 2.5ff.) for a more detailed analysis of attendance statistics across the UK and Europe in the last 25 years.

3 See Goodhew's work (2012) for a description of the UK context, and (2017) for a global Anglican perspective. Alongside Rob Barward-Symmons, Goodhew has also charted the rise of new churches in the North East since 1980 (2015b), but as the criteria for inclusion in this study include a church needing to meet for worship every week, many fresh expressions are discounted from it.

4 *The Declaration of Ascent*: www.churchofengland.org/prayer-worship/worship/texts/mvcontents/preface.aspx; accessed 24 June 2016.

5 'What is a Fresh Expression?': https://freshexpressions.org.uk/about/what-is-a-fresh-expression; accessed 21 Sept. 2017.

6 'Quick Look A02 – Mission Context': http://freshexpressions.org.uk/resources-3/quick-look-guides/quick-look-a02-mission-context; accessed 21 Sept. 2017.

7 You can also download a description of this process, *How to Start a Fresh Expression of Church*, from 'Tried and Tested Resources': https://freshexpressions.org.uk/resources-3/tried-and-tested-resources; accessed 26 Aug. 2017.

8 See www.theuglyducklingcompany.com/Table-talk.html; accessed 14 Feb. 2018.

2

Can a single-demographic church work?

We had made a good start. Having built relationships and engaged in listening exercises, some of our own activities had begun, which opened up new avenues for engaging the community. The active listening we undertook was crucial to discerning what might be useful. However, another important source of discernment were the skills, passions and interests that were held within the core team. I have already mentioned how the Monday Night Football group was one of the first things to get started, the impetus for which came both from my desire to play friendly football regularly and from others who had also articulated that desire. It would have been difficult to try and launch a ministry when no one in the core team was either skilled for it or passionate about it, however much it might be needed. The make-up of the core team was crucial. The impetus for our next activity also came from both the needs of the community and the team's make-up. At the time, all of us had young families. This fact was to shape much of what we did in the first couple of years.

We had noticed that the demographic of the development consisted predominantly of families with young children. A significant number were pre-school aged, yet there were no activities on the development for this age group. Added to this, with a large number of families being dual-income commuters, up until the point of having children they had often not invested in relationships with neighbours. Before having children their social circles would be formed from the workplace and through existing friendships with people in other towns and cities. After the first child was born and the support given from visiting family in the initial weeks was over, when grandparents had returned home, often the new mothers would find themselves feeling isolated, with a new baby and little friendship support around them. Geographically, St Crispin's sat right in between children's and Sure Start centres in other areas, resulting in a long walk or short drive to get to either. Some parents took advantage of these but many of the mums we met were eager for some sort of a group within walking distance of their homes.

A few months earlier we had become acquainted with a volunteer children's worker from another church who was also a trained teacher of baby sign language. The idea behind this is that babies from about six months onwards can learn to communicate their basic needs through simple signs before their speech has developed. Using these, they can easily ask for something to eat or drink, say if they have hurt themselves or have a wet nappy. It is not foolproof, but it is intended to reduce frustrations that come when babies are unable to express what they want. Towards the end of our first year in post, we advertised and ran two of these six-session courses from our house, which then enabled us to get to know new people from the development. After the second of these, the signing teacher moved on to find other sources of income, but the precedent that our house was one in which we welcomed the community had been set. From this group we began a regular drop-in for parents and babies to get to know one another and to receive support and advice from health visitors, child nutritionists and other early-years professionals who stopped in from time to time.

Meanwhile, Kate, Helen and my wife Sarah, who had been meeting to read the Bible and pray together, were joined by Laura, another member of the core team who had just had a baby. This informal gathering became a regular commitment, which would grow as they were later joined by others from outside the core team: one of the mums who had been on the baby signing course and another dechurched mother who lived down the road. As the kids got older we provided age-appropriate Bible input for them too. This ministry became known as Bible and Bubbles. The members developed an honesty and vulnerability, giving and receiving love and support. This group was to be where people grew in their faith the most.

The groups mentioned above were mostly about women and young children. Family activities were the natural place to start due to the make-up both of the community and of our core team. For the sport-loving men we started Monday Night Football, which led into starting the Curry and Questions group mentioned in the previous chapter. Also in the first 18 months we started a book group, which was intended for both men and women but in practice was mostly attended by women. After building deeper relationships with male neighbours, a men-only book group was begun. We met in the pub, drank beer and read non-fiction as well as fiction. In both these groups we took it in turns to choose what book to read, which resulted in our discussing a wide variety of styles and quality of literature. Depending on the book, we were able to explore spiritual questions arising from the writing.

Each of these groups began from discerning the needs or desires of a particular strand of the community. They were targeted at specific groups, resulting in their being fairly homogeneous in their make-up: the book group was mostly women; Bible and Bubbles was entirely mums; Curry and Questions was made up exclusively of dads. In fact even our Sunday gatherings, when they started, were made up mostly of families with young children. In the rest of this chapter I will explore two questions. First, given that many fresh expressions begin in a similar manner to ours, focusing on one demographic or interest group, are they a legitimate and biblical place to start when wanting to plant new congregations? Second, was the seemingly homogeneous nature of the groups we had begun a problem? Weren't we supposed to be the body of Christ, representing human diversity? Instead, had we ended up with just a small group of like-minded people in the same stage of life?

Is this a biblical approach to planting churches?

Just prior to his ascension, Jesus left his disciples with the command that they should witness to him 'in Jerusalem, and in all Judea and Samaria, and to the ends of the earth' (Acts 1.8). These three stages can be seen as pattern for the book of Acts, as the Spirit drives and leads the first disciples further out from the city of Jerusalem. The first seven chapters of Acts are set in Jerusalem, with a description of the Spirit coming to the gathered crowds at Pentecost and the founding of the first church. Here, mission was mainly focused on the Jews and God-fearing Gentiles who had gathered for the festival. After Stephen was martyred, the church faced persecution and all except the apostles were scattered 'throughout Judea and Samaria' (Acts 8.1), with the result that mission moved on to include Samaritans. Shortly after, the mission extended to the Gentiles; Peter received a clear call from God to go to Cornelius, a Roman centurion, then Saul and Barnabas were sent off on their first missionary journey and found that many non-Jews wanted to follow Christ (Acts 13). During their second journey, after several false starts, Saul – now called Paul and travelling with Silas and Timothy – was given a vision of a man of Macedonia beckoning him, Silas and Timothy over the northern Aegean Sea to southern Europe.

These three stages can be considered to be three major acts of Spirit. It was the Spirit who was influential at Pentecost, the Spirit who gave the Christians power to witness to those they met outside of Jerusalem after the persecution and scattering that followed the stoning of Stephen, and the Spirit who revealed that vision from heaven of clean and unclean foods to Peter, calling him to go to Cornelius. It was Jesus himself who appeared to Saul on the Damascus road and inspired the Antioch church to send Paul and Barnabas out from there. Any pioneering to new people and new places in Acts was Spirit-led.

The British New Testament scholar Richard Bauckham notes that this process was also scriptural for them at the time (2011, pp. 205–6); this three-stage act of the Holy Spirit did not cause the first Christians to go beyond the remit of Scripture. Of course, at the time the only Scripture they had was the Old Testament, but this threefold movement is clearly set out. Stephen's speech before his stoning in Acts 7 can at first sight appear a little random within the narrative of Acts. He spends very little time talking about Jesus, concentrating instead on how God related to Israel before the establishment of the Temple. The climax of his speech is about how God does not live in the Temple but how the whole earth belongs to him. Just like their Hebrew ancestors who ignored God, worshipped the golden calf and persecuted the prophets, now too, Stephen says, the Jewish people are resisting the Holy Spirit. This got him stoned and Christians were forced to leave Jerusalem, where the Temple, and thus the focus of Jewish worship, was located. Up until that point, much of the new Christians' meeting and teaching had occurred within the Temple courts. By being forced out of Jerusalem, the early Church had to adapt their patterns of meeting and worship. The immediate effect of this was that the reach of the gospel expanded to include Samaritans (Acts 8.4–25), a eunuch (Acts 8.26–40), God-fearing Gentiles (Acts 10) and Gentiles (Acts 13ff.). This same pattern can be found in Isaiah 56, when God's word goes out to outcasts of Israel, eunuchs, foreigners who join themselves to the Lord, and finally to all the world. Christianity had to move beyond the context of the Jewish Temple in order to fulfil the scriptural mandate set out in Isaiah. Stephen's speech points the way for the mission that is to come. Bauckham suggests that in Acts, through Stephen's speech, Luke is emphasizing how these pioneering developments were new but did not take the mission of God beyond Scripture. It may have been a departure from tradition but it was not outside the scriptural mandate of God.

In these three acts of the Spirit resulting in the mission to the Jews, Samaritans and Gentiles, Freddy Hedley sees three different shapes to the church communities that formed, each of which has relevance today (2010, p. 29). The first shape, as seen in the Jerusalem church, could be called an attractional or collated church. Jerusalem was a strategic place to be, receiving visitors from a wide area due to its being a centre of pilgrimage. A church in Jerusalem could be very influential as people came, heard the gospel and then took it out with them wherever they were to go. The end of the book of Acts describes Paul finally arriving in Rome (Acts 28.14). According to his letter to the Romans, he had been intending to visit for some time but did not make it until near the end of his life. In Acts there was no mention of a church in Rome until this final chapter. There was also no mention of a mission to Rome. Yet Paul knew that a church had been started in Rome, and had written a letter a few years earlier to Christians there. Who started the church in Rome, and when? Looking back to Acts 2.10, we see that visitors from Rome were among the many nations represented in Jerusalem when the Holy Spirit descended. Could they have been among the first Christians who then took the gospel back? There is evidence from an edict of the Emperor Claudius that Christianity could have been present in Rome as early as AD 41, just nine years after the resurrection, so it is not unthinkable that converted Jews living in Rome had received the Spirit at Pentecost in Jerusalem.[1]

We still need churches like the Jerusalem church today, in strategic centres with a continual flow of people. There are many global cities in the world today with a multi-ethnic, multicultural, and multinational population. People may settle in a city for a few years for education or for a specific job before relocating again or moving back to their place of origin. Only one of the UK's ten megachurches – defined as having over 2,000 distinct worshippers on a Sunday (Thumma and Travis, 2007) – is located outside London.[2] All the megachurches in the capital are significantly multi-ethnic or, predominantly, single-ethnicity African pentecostal churches. The phenomenon of megachurches only really comes about because of the global nature of the city itself. Even in large churches with fewer than 2,000 members, there is often a strong focus on international welcome, especially in cities with a high population of students. The hope of such ministries is that visitors from all over the world will come to study for a few years, hear the gospel and then return to their home nation as Christians. These cities are strategic centres for attractional models of church similar to the church in Jerusalem.

After the persecution, the Jerusalem Christians were scattered into the surrounding area. Here a second shape emerged as they had to start accommodating to different aspects of culture. Hedley calls this the dispersed church (2010, p. 29). Churches were different sizes. They often comprised small groups meeting in homes, and some of these may have been monocultural. Occasionally they may have come together across a city for a larger gathering. Paul's letter to the Galatians indicates that ethnic groups met separately (Gal. 2.11–13), yet they also must have come together since we are told that Paul confronted Peter – about eating only with Jews – 'in front of them all' (Gal. 2.14). This pattern of small monocultural groups can also be seen in the church in Antioch, the city in which believers were first called Christians. It was a large and important city in the Roman Empire, with 18 distinct ethnic quarters. It is likely that there were small groups in each quarter. It was also a church with a continual sending out and receiving back of small groups of between two and five people for missional purposes. Hence their focus was both on building up the people in Antioch and building the kingdom elsewhere. Large towns or cities today can have a mixture of both attractional churches and dispersed churches, which serve specific areas of the city.

The final shape, which Hedley calls the mobilized or emerging church (2010, p. 62), is where the church adapted to the surrounding culture depending on the characteristics of the area. Although the process was slightly different in each place, the strategy centred around finding people of peace. In Philippi (Acts 16.11–15), Paul spent several days in the city before finding such a person, Lydia, at a place of prayer outside the city. Her whole household believed and was baptized, and very quickly her home became Paul's base of operations in Philippi. In Berea (Acts 17.10–14), Paul and Silas were welcomed at the synagogue, and consequently many of the worshippers believed. In Athens, Paul discussed the faith in the synagogue with the Jews as well as in the marketplace with the Gentiles, which was their place for debate and exchange of ideas (Acts 17.16–34). After this he was invited to speak at the Areopagus, the central council, where some sneered, others wanted to discuss further and still others believed (Acts 17.32–34). In Ephesus, Paul arrived to find believers already there, although they had not yet received the Spirit. There is no single pattern for the churches that emerged. In each place Paul and his companions began by finding people of peace; the churches formed around them. They were often structured around small groups, based in homes, and were sometimes connected through networks, visits, letters or central gatherings. For example, in the church in Rome there was diversity: the list mentioned in Romans 16 includes slave, Greek and Latin (Roman) names (Jewett, 2007, p. 63). There is no evidence they met together but Paul's letter, which is addressed to 'all in Rome' (Rom. 1.7), indicates there must have been a connection of some kind. In Corinth there is evidence from Paul's letters that they met together as a larger group (1 Cor. 14.23). Churches based in larger homes may have included relatives of the host family as well as workers, slaves and tenants, all in the same congregation.

In this final shape of mobilized or emerging churches, we cannot see a specific pattern to the form they took but we can see similarities in the way they were created. The pioneer sought out the people of peace in the community – those who were open to hearing and receiving the gospel – and church formed around them. There were key differences in each place that were context-dependent, but also notable similarities that could be seen in the values of the gospel and the importance of Christian community. One of Hedley's key phrases through-out his book is: 'you inherit values and pioneer form' (2010, p. 65). This would appear to fit. The shape of the church in each location changed according to the people and the con-text that were found, but each remained distinctly Christian in character. From this reading of the early Church in Acts, there appears to be a biblical precedent for creating networks of context-specific groups which, while different in their form, are nevertheless distinctly Christian in their nature. Both the dispersed and mobilized/emerging shapes are particularly rel-evant to the fresh expressions discussion, and seem to give a biblical basis for a contextual approach to church planting.

Can a non-diverse group legitimately be called church?

If the approach to church planting can be seen to be biblical, what about the nature of the church that is formed? Don't new ecclesial communities simply create groups of Christians who are culturally and socially exactly the same? Can a church just for knitters, teenagers or middle-class professionals with young children legitimately be called church? In the book of Revelation there is a beautiful vision of people from every nation, tongue and tribe gathered around Christ's throne worshipping God (Rev. 7.9). If this is a vision of heaven, should all churches strive to echo it, being made up of people with a diversity of ages, ethnicities and interests? Or should a church reflect the make-up of the wider society in which it sits? When this does happen, it is a beautiful sight indeed. However, fresh expressions of church have come under scrutiny due to the belief that they are producing the exact opposite of this diverse vision of Revelation. They have been started for goths, for parents and pre-schoolers, for the retired, for surfers. Of course, none of these churches would say they are catering for these groups to the exclusion of all others, but in doing church in a way that specific groups can relate to more easily, it is inevitable that people outside these subcultures or age-demographics do not find their way into such churches. Hence a church can become somewhat monocultural or homogeneous in its make-up.

Mission-Shaped Church picked up that this was happening and turned to the twentieth-century missionary and missiologist Donald McGavran for insight. Based on his observations as a missionary in India, McGavran noticed that the gospel tended to spread most easily among people who were alike:

> People like to become Christians without crossing racial/ linguistic/class/cultural barriers . . . Culturally they remain the same, and tend to gather with others from the same culture who share their faith. It is this sameness that marks the group as 'homogenous'. (McGavran, 1955; cited in *Mission-Shaped Church*, p. 108)

This has become known as the 'homogeneous unit principle'. Following this principle it would make sense to begin with the culture and interests of specific people-groups in forming new contextual churches, as many fresh expressions have tended to do.

In the years after the publication of the *Mission-Shaped Church* report, while fresh expressions were beginning to have a significant impact on the Church in Britain, several books and articles were written critiquing the theology and principles on which they are based. Shortly after the report came out, John Hull, who is broadly in favour of fresh expressions, wrote a booklet challenging some of the theological underpinnings of the report (Hull, 2006). John Milbank and Martin Percy were also active in writing articles and chapters of edited books examining the underlying theology (see Milbank, 2008; Percy, 2008). Notably, Andrew Davison and Alison Milbank's *For the Parish* (2010) purported to be a defence of parish ministry but reads as a scathing critique of fresh expressions. One of the common strands of critique from these authors is their dissatisfaction with the homogeneous unit principle and the perception that many fresh expressions are monocultural.

Their main critique is that segregation is psychologically unhealthy for the individual and for Christian society, as people remain isolated in the small enclaves they emerged from. Creating a church for one subculture means that those who become Christian never get to experience the broadness and fullness of diversity across God's kingdom. Church should be fully 'one' – that is, united – and 'catholic', embracing the full diversity of creation. Davison and Milbank claim that the homogeneous unit principle – and therefore fresh expressions – created communities that remain isolated in their segregation (2010, p. 17). John Hull even goes so far as to say that the principle that subcultures develop best separately from others is the basic idea behind apartheid (2006, p. 14), which, when applied systemically in South Africa, led to the oppression of many ethnic groups.

As a contrast to such isolated and monocultural forms of church, John Milbank paints an idealized picture of the geographical parish church consisting of a diverse human community, collaborating together, full of different gifts, in one location (2008, pp. 117ff.). Like the other authors who critique fresh expressions on this point, he argues that mission is best achieved out of the parish church, and that homogeneous churches cannot be real church:

> One can't set up a church in a café among a gang of youths who like skateboarding because all this does is promote skateboarding and dysfunctional escapist maleness, along with that type of private but extra-ecclesial security that is offered by the notion of 'being saved'. The real, universal Church is found always paradoxically in one place, within one circumscribed boundary and in one sacred, consecrated building. (2008, p. 124)

While, curiously, Milbank relates the presence of church with a building, something the New Testament does not do, this idealized view of the parish is also narrow in its scope. Despite seeking to articulate a vision of a broad and diverse parish church, it neglects the breadth of style, tradition, background and diversity that exists in the Church of England and in the wider Church – of whatever denomination – in Britain. Presumably the authors would have similar questions over single-ethnicity churches such as Trinity Baptist Church, home to a gathered community of around 800 worshippers of Ghanaian descent in Croydon, or Jesus House, a predominantly Nigerian congregation of around 3,000 located in Brent Cross. These churches illustrate that the homogeneous unit principle may be effective in establishing new churches.

The reality is that parish churches usually do not conform to the idealized picture that is desired either: they can be extremely homogeneous themselves. Many tend to be predominantly elderly, female, white and middle-class. Even in areas where there is a high proportion of youth or working-class people, they seem only to attract the older or more middle-class members of the community. Others are particularly conservative or liberal in theology, some operate in a way that unintentionally excludes those with little formal education, while others reflect a specific taste in music that may be accessible only to some subcultures. For example, the recently planted Resource Church in

Durham diocese, St Georges Gateshead, which began with a planting team of around 15 people who moved the 130 miles from Sheffield, grew into a regular congregation of over a hundred in under eight months. This is to be commended, but even here we need to acknowledge both a specific taste in music that will be attractive to some people but not others, and a young-family dynamic that may result in a lower proportion of the elderly attending compared to the surrounding community. Similarly, the parish church with the robed choir and sung eucharistic settings will engage some but not others.

These trends reflect a growing social fragmentation within society. While the modern era, which extended into the second half of the twentieth century, can be characterized by certainty, scientific optimism and truth, the postmodern era has given way to more freedom of choice, increased individualization, alongside the opportunity to construct identities. Class, religion and gender are no longer the foundations on which identity is built; all aspects of a person's being, including lifestyle, interests, tastes, religious and political views, sexual preferences and even gender itself can be appropriated into a unique individualized self-identity. Increased consumer choice extends far beyond what food or clothes to buy, to affect even where we get our news and thus how we learn about and see the world. In this context, communities, which can now exist in physical or virtual space, often spring up not on geographical lines but, as the sociologist Zygmunt Bauman claims, suddenly and fleetingly, based on common interest, identity or purpose. Bauman claims that just one commonality is enough to form a community in our postmodern times, other differences metaphorically being left at the door by members of that community for the duration of their participation in it (2000, pp. 199–201). But such advances have come at a cost. The enduring qualities of modernist communities have passed, giving way to uncertainty, while at the same time offering great opportunities. As Carlo Bordini writes, responding to Bauman:

[community] is not the place you belong to, where you were born and where you were educated and where you go back to in order to find yourself. That form of *communitas* is obsolete, it is part of cultural archaeology . . . Today the community is a weak bond, more fragile and temporary than any other economic or structural social bond, but capable of great performance. It has shaken off most of the influences of the past and has assumed a freedom of action over a long distance, which makes it the most versatile and useful tool of social relations. (2016, pp. 96–7)

Pete Ward's response to postmodernity's social changes is to suggest that the church needs to be more creative, or 'liquid', as a result. Forms of church based on modernist certainties no longer hold the same sway in society. Characteristics of these liquid churches will include a focus on relationship, participation by all rather than top-down leadership (thus releasing creativity), and softer boundaries around the edges determining who belongs (Ward, 2002, pp. 46–8). New ecclesial communities that are more flexible and fluid, and can cater for commonalities found in individualized identities, are therefore ideally suited to mission in a fragmented society. They are simply an extension of the church's mission to those who are not being reached by parish life in certain areas.

Despite this talk of homogeneity, it is worth noting that fresh expressions congregations can be remarkably diverse. They do not all deserve to be called monocultural; many are not niche churches but serve the resident population in an area. Despite our tendency towards serving those with children, that was what we were trying to do at Berrywood. Even those fresh expressions that are based around an interest are often diverse in gender, personality types and age range (Lings, 2012, p. 172).

I have already argued above how the New Testament church had aspects of homogeneity. The early churches in each of Antioch's 18 cultural quarters would have drawn in families and networks from the nearby streets. Each house church may have been fairly monocultural, differing from those based in other quarters. Paul is clear in his writing that he did not tolerate divisions between cultures: 'There is neither Jew nor Gentile, neither slave nor free, nor is there male and female, for you are all one in Christ Jesus' (Gal. 3.28). Similarly, diversity and difference is celebrated in his body-of-Christ analogy (1 Cor. 12). Members of the Church need each other, and without each other we have a silly collection of eyes or noses that cannot be called a body. However, in Antioch they also met together as the whole church in the city from time to time. This would have been true in the church in Galatia too, and in Corinth (see Gal. 2.12–14; 1 Cor. 14.22–23). From this it seems that the early Church was comfortable with monocultural groups so long as this monoculture did not come to define the Christians in that place. The primary identity was always based on Christ. Occasional city-wide gatherings inclusive of the whole diversity of Christians in the city would have cemented this belief.

Moynagh is pragmatic when it comes to this issue (2012, pp. 171–2), arguing that aspects of homogeneity in a church can be important to allow networking within the culture for the sake of passing on the gospel message. In his most recent book he moves the conversation on from the somewhat controversial principle of McGavran by talking about 'affinity groups' rather than 'homogeneous units' (2017, pp. 219–20). This recognizes that McGavran was mostly talking about what he had observed in other cultures regarding language, class and race divisions, whereas now the principle is also used in relation to other commonalities, such as a shared interest or line of work, and therefore can avoid the accusation of apartheid. In Western contemporary society, people are now able to choose who their friends are to a greater degree than in the past. Naturally they choose others with whom they have something in common; they form affinity groups. Therefore, moving on from the homogeneous unit principle, the principle of affinity groups can be utilized for the sake of mission. In fact some of the more homogeneous contextual churches in Acts would have grown out of local missional activity in each cultural quarter. However, Moynagh does stress the importance both of networks within affinity groups, which draw people in, and networks between groups, which link different affinity groups together. With these networks, even homogeneous affinity groups can celebrate the diversity of culture that God has created (2017, pp. 233ff.), and can claim to be 'one in Christ Jesus'.

Applying this back into fresh expressions, new ecclesial communities can be focused around affinity groups for pragmatic missional reasons. What happens after conversion in an individual is that identity with the cultural group may remain, but becomes secondary as the person is incorporated into the family of God. Whatever their initial identity was, there is now a new priority. Surfers can remain surfers but when they come to faith their primary identity is 'in Christ'; Goths can remain goths but also belong to something larger. People do not lose their original identity but are joined to a wider family. This does not mean that new ecclesial communities need to change their missional approach to intentionally draw others in from outside of their existing circles, but seeing as those within fresh expressions are members of the body of Christ, it is wise to encourage wider connections with those from other expressions of church, both traditional and fresh. To go back to Hull's accusation: this is not apartheid if the intention is to forge links with other Christians from different subcultures.

Ultimately this leads us to a pattern of different forms of church working alongside each other for mutual benefit, in what Rowan Williams, Archbishop of Canterbury when *Mission-Shaped Church* was published, called the 'mixed economy'. *Mission-Shaped Church* describes an 'active partnership' of fresh expressions and traditional churches working together across a parish or deanery (*Mission-Shaped Church*, p. xi). Together they can overcome the limitations of culturally homogeneous churches.

One limitation of the single-church parish model is that when someone leaves the church there can be nowhere else for them to go. A mixed-economy approach can help with this. In the church in which I served my curacy, my training incumbent wanted to make sure the 'back door' to the church was closed. We were very good at welcoming people into our congregation but there was a sense that sometimes people would slip out again quietly after a few years. Naturally the vicar was keen to hang on to them. In their study of reasons why people leave church, *Gone for Good*, Leslie Francis and Philip Richter acknowledge that in fact the back door to a church will always exist and it may be impossible to close it completely; people leave for all kinds of reasons, not all of them negative. However, they redeem the idea of the back door so that instead of exiting indefinitely, members can transition on to a congregation of a different flavour. They use the concept of multiplex churches, where several congregations of different types coexist alongside one another and where a freedom of movement exists between them, depending on an individual's life-stage, identity, ideas, needs and preferences: '[The multiplex idea] encourages churches in a locality to think of each other not as competitors but as collaborators, referring potential church-leavers on to other partner churches who can better meet their needs' (2007, p. 309). They see their vision as being greater than that described by *Mission-Shaped Church*, although in reality they have described the mixed economy at its best, serving both existing churchgoers and those who are not yet connected. It is easy to see how a network of traditional and new contextual churches working together across an area can be a blessing both to the area and to one another. Instead of leaving for good, those using the back door may be persuaded to try a different style of congregation in the locality. Similarly, those who come to faith through a culture-specific fresh expression may wish to transition on to a more traditional form of church. Working together in a mixed economy removes some of the limitations of homogeneous congregations, seeing diversity across the wider whole, and enables traditional congregations to be challenged by the creativity and missional energy of pioneering ventures.

Looking at fresh expressions as a whole also reveals the diversity of the body of Christ. Andy Wier of the Church Army conducted quantitative research into 66 fresh expressions across six dioceses, comparing them against a control sample of 12 traditional churches across three dioceses. The main focus of his research was to ascertain the backgrounds of attendees in fresh expressions in terms of previous church involvement: are fresh expressions actually reaching the unchurched as they were intended? Out of this data also came information about age demographics. Taken as a whole, the fresh expressions were considerably more diverse in age range than the sample of traditional churches, where 65 per cent of attendees were over the age of 55. Within fresh expressions, 78 per cent were under the age of 54, more closely matching the demographics of the population as a whole (2016, pp. 43, 54).[3] Of course, individually, the fresh expression may have concentrated specifically on ministering to children, young adults or another subculture, but taken together, Wier's data indicates that fresh expressions are significantly better at engaging with certain parts of the population than are many traditional churches. The question should therefore not be about how homogeneous a church may or may not be, as clearly both fresh expressions and traditional churches can be homogeneous in different ways, but about whether the Church as a whole is engaging fruitfully with all sections of society.

So to answer my questions above, new ecclesial communities can be seen as a biblical approach to planting churches. Although clearly the language of fresh expressions or contextual church was not around at the time, some of the approaches that can be seen in the early Church in Acts are reflected in the approaches taken to engage with unreached subcultures and different demographics in contemporary times. Likewise we see aspects of homogeneity and diversity within the early Church; therefore forming fresh new contextual churches around a homogeneous subculture should not act as a barrier to mission, although bridging links to other Christian communities should be encouraged. What we were doing at Berrywood in forming different groups for various interests could be considered both biblical and pragmatic. Having done this, and having made meaningful connections with a significant number of residents from the housing development, we were ready to think about how to worship within our context.

Notes

1 The evidence concerns an edict from the Emperor Claudius expelling the Jews from Jerusalem. The Roman historian Suetonius mentions this edict in relation to 'disturbances at the instigation of Chrestus', which many have taken to mean a conflict within the Jewish community over the nature of Christ. This edict can be dated – using the writing of Suetonius and another Roman historian, Cassius Dio – to either AD 41 or 49, or two separate edicts in both these years. The timeline and interpretation of events is far from clear, as Greg MaGee relates (MaGee, 2008). Either of these timelines predates Paul's appearance in Rome, and could suggest – albeit far from conclusively – that Roman Jews converted at Pentecost may have returned and started spreading the gospel, resulting in a network of Christian communities across the city by the time Paul wrote his letter.

2 A megachurch has been defined as a Protestant church that draws more than 2,000 distinct attendees across all their weekend services (Thumma and Travis, 2007, pp. xviii–xxi). This has become the standard definition used in the study of megachurches. It does, however, notably neglect worship services that take place midweek, and doesn't address Catholic congregations.

3 At the 2011 census, 54 per cent of the population of the UK was under 54 years of age (2011 Census, Table 1: Usual Resident Population by Five-Year Age Group and Sex, United Kingdom and Constituent Countries, *Office for National Statistics*: www.ons.gov.uk /ons/rel/census/2011-census/population-and-household-estimates-for -the-united-kingdom/rft-table-1-census-2011.xls; accessed 7 July 2017).

3

What makes a church?

We had reached the stage at which we wanted to start gathering regularly together. The core team was small but committed. Some of us were going to other churches' Sunday-morning services but had begun to feel that this small group was now our main worshipping community. For some in our group, particularly those who had unbelieving partners, it was difficult to get to Sunday-morning worship in other churches. And we also wanted a meeting with which the growing number of neighbours on the housing development who were interested in our work could engage. But what should our gatherings look like? How do we adapt Christian worship to the context we are in? Should we aim to create a gathering that will resource and equip us in our mission, or should it be accessible enough to invite others to? What should be done, and crucially what should not be done during our time together? And fundamentally, would this make us 'church'? What elements are needed to create an authentic church? These last two questions are often levelled at fresh expressions and are therefore the questions I will investigate in this chapter. In particular I will assess some of the different forms that fresh expressions of church have taken, and ask what elements need to be present for them to be authentic church. The answer to these questions can have a bearing on how to define success, which I will address later in the book.

At this point in the development of Berrywood Church we had engaged in a number of community initiatives and missional projects, but I would not yet have said we were church. However, I had felt that it was important to have the word 'church' in our name, so that the community would know we were a Christian group intending to gather together. But what makes a church?

What does contextual church look like?

Contextual churches set up under the Fresh Expressions umbrella vary hugely in approach and practice. Their range of core activities similarly varies, leading to difficulty in defining what is and is not church. In one sense I could argue that the answer to the question 'Are they church?' doesn't matter so long as the fresh expression is engaging with those who are otherwise not being reached by traditional church, and is enabling them to start or continue a journey of faith. But on the other hand, if we want to create communities that are not stepping stones but can function as a believer's primary church community, then the answer to this question is important, as it leads us towards important elements and principles that need to be in place. These principles need to be broad enough not to inhibit the development of a new congregation that may look radically different from what we are used to seeing. For example, Tubestation, which serves the surfing community in Cornwall by offering tuition and equipment hire, adapted a former Methodist chapel by installing a café and skateboard ramp in the chancel. From their activities in this subculture, relationships were formed and weekly worship and small groups emerged.[1] Knit and Natter on the Wirral is a 'knitting church', where members gather for company, support and prayer while knitting. They were founded with a key value of serving others, and accordingly all that they knit goes to those in need.[2] On the surface we may ask the question: 'How can a knitting group be church?' Yet they have seen several people come to faith and have even had baptisms during their sessions. Many who come regard this as their worshipping community. In Coventry and Cambridge, two fresh expressions served those from the Goth culture. Their practices may have looked more like a recognizable church than my previous two examples, as they met in ecclesial buildings and used traditional liturgy, but they too were tailored to the needs of the subculture they seek to serve.[3] Revd Marcus Ramshaw, who instigated The Goth Eucharist in Cambridge, featured in the second Fresh Expressions DVD, remarks that they offer a safe space for a subculture often marginalized by mainstream society, and a forum for issues common to the Goth community to be discussed, such as self-harm or depression.[4] These are just three examples of fresh expressions set up around a subculture or pre-existing community. They serve people from these subcultures who often come together from a network of relationships that cover a wide geographical area.

The *Mission-Shaped Church* report identified a list of 12 different categories of fresh expression (p. 44). Examples within each category have some common attributes or characteristics in their shape or style of gathering. The first type identified are alternative-worship communities who experiment with the tradition, form and structure of worship. Grace, based in St Mary's Church, Ealing, has been running for over 25 years, since before the term 'fresh expressions of church' was coined. Their experimentation has led to many different forms over the years but often includes a community meal and attention to spiritual practices. Some new monastic movements would also fall into this category. They use a rhythm of life and are attentive to tradition, drawing on the ancient spiritual sources of monasticism. Some of them live in residential community, others are dispersed communities that follow a rule of life, coming together periodically (such as the Northumbria Community, who maintain a retreat house in Felton, Northumberland).[5] The Moot Community, who meet in central London, provide a wide variety of spiritual groups and communal worship through the week. They draw in members from across London who are all committed to a rhythm of life in one of three different ways of belonging.[6]

The second type of fresh expression, base ecclesial communities, originally sprung up in poorer communities of Latin America, where the Catholic Church is traditionally dominant. Out of a Church with a strong hierarchical structure, and from which fellowship is considered to be mediated by the sacraments, base communities grew from the bottom up, out of the local context in order to serve it, but remained Catholic. One of the pioneer theologians from this movement, Leonardo Boff, described these churches as places where congregations form around close-knit community rather than hierarchy, where people know one another by name and where each member has influence over the direction of the group. Communities love and support each other in the living-out of gospel values, and by promoting equality among members (Boff, 1986, pp. 1–13). Translated into contemporary British society, base communities have come to mean those formed around these values, which reach out to a specific culture and have a strong sense of identity. Tubestation, the church for surfers mentioned above, and Legacy XS, a church that operates from its own purpose-built skateboard park in Essex, would be examples of this type.[7] What they do when they gather would depend on the culture and make-up of the base community.

Café churches, the third type of fresh expressions identified, can be either geographically or network based. They tend to meet outside of church buildings and emphasize discussion and relationship. One of the examples highlighted in the Fresh Expressions material is the Taste and See café in Kidsgrove, Staffordshire.[8] The local churches had noted that there was a missing generation of those in their twenties and thirties across all the churches in the town, and wanted to work together to reach them. They also noted that although coffee culture had impacted society in general, there was little in the way of coffee shops in the town. So they worked together to set up a café from which they serve the community and build relationships. A small community formed, which started to worship together in an informal, interactive way. Other café churches have used existing coffee shops, such as the Lounge in Woodbridge, Suffolk, who meet in the local branch of Costa. Still others have recreated a café-style atmosphere in another building, such as River Community Church near Telford, who meet in a village hall.

Some fresh expressions arise from acts of service to others. The Lighthouse in Bristol sprung out of a desire to effect community transformation on needy housing estates.[9] One of their first activities was a community clean-up, which then led to community meals, sharing of testimonies, and discipleship. This project was run entirely by volunteers. The Urban Expressions organization, which predates the Fresh Expressions movement, seeks to plant churches in deprived areas through incarnational ministry. Their first church, Cable Street (which has now merged with other Urban Expression plants to serve a larger area), saw one couple move into the Tower Hamlets area of London to build relationships and engage in community transformation. There are now many such examples in the UK, with other organizations, such as Eden, starting from similar ideals.

Network churches consist of many interlinked groups all committed to a different aspect of life. Sometimes these groups are called missional communities and run a specific ministry, or are dedicated to a subculture or interest. In Exeter Network Church, some groups are organized by interest (such as football or sewing), some by ministry (such as healing on the streets) and some by life-stage.[10] In the beginning the different nodes of the network all met together once a month for a celebration gathering and to provide each other with mutual support. Now the Sunday gatherings happen most weeks. In the case of Cheltenham Network Church, their networks include a book club, a board-games group, those who support an overseas mission, a prayer group for businessmen and a group for those who work in the voluntary sector.[11] They meet every Sunday but it is the network groups that are the core of their identity.

Mission-Shaped Church also identified cell churches, multiple and midweek congregations, churches that sprung out of school ministries, seeker church (in which services are presented in a jargon-free way to help those new to faith), traditional church plants, and youth congregations. Two more – church for pre-schoolers and for families of young children – were added to the list of 12 after *Mission-Shaped Church* was published (Croft, 2008a, p. 9). Messy Church would fit into the last category.

It is easy to look at the categories above and question whether some of them are authentic fresh expressions or indeed authentic church. Are they suitably contextual to be called a fresh expression, and are they suitably ecclesial to be called church? Some look more like church than others. Ian Mobsby, who was the leader of the Moot new monastic community and one of the first to write about evaluating fresh expressions, claims that only three out of the 14 categories – new monastic communities, café church and network churches – are authentically contextual. The others all exhibit an inherited church structure of some kind (2007, p. 31). Mobsby's thoughts would indicate, if we were to use the Fresh Expressions definition strictly, that many groups cannot authentically be called fresh expressions. I would certainly question why traditional church plants are included as fresh expressions, without denying the great effectiveness they can have in the right places. But simply having elements of church structure does not disqualify an instance of church from being a fresh expression. The key is contextuality: 'Is this shape of church right for these people in this place?' For example, on the surface the 'Midweeker' congregation at St Jude's, the charismatic evangelical church in Plymouth, looks like a traditional congregation, but it arose from Fresh Expressions principles. When the vicar and a small group started doing the Mission-Shaped Ministry course run by the diocese, they recognized that there was a missing generation in their church. Many unchurched elderly people lived in the parish and the church was not meeting their needs. After prayerful listening to the local community a congregation was started, which combined close fellowship with short traditional worship and an emphasis on eating together and other social events.[12] It often includes BCP communion but is fresh because it has emerged from contextual thinking to reach an unreached culture in that parish.

These categories and associated examples offer lots of ideas for ways to structure church. Which structure would we go for in our context? Simply copying another church structure and lifting it into another context would not be the way to proceed. The structure and ideas from River Community Church and other fresh expressions were important, but they wouldn't necessarily lift to a new situation. One of the keys to fresh expressions is contextuality, and we would have to do our own work in determining what might be appropriate in our context.

What is church?

Another question on our minds was, even if we did begin contextual worship, how might our missional engagements become church? What elements would we need? In order to be accepted into traditional denominations as congregations in themselves, not as stepping stones for mission, fresh expressions would need to demonstrate that they are suitably ecclesial – are they a legitimate form of church? So what makes a church? The trouble with this question is that there are so many places to begin. The shape of the church has varied throughout the ages, according to theology, context and tradition. All church traditions have the elements of Scripture, community and fellowship, Eucharist and a dependence on the Spirit to some degree, but each places its priority differently, which then affects its shape. For example, in the charismatic and pentecostal traditions the presence of the Spirit is the defining mark of the church, over and above the sacraments or preaching. The Holy Spirit indwells each believer and enables them to encounter God. Spiritual gifts and experiences are given to deepen their faith, to build up the body of the Church and empower them for service. Often the worship service is shaped around the divine encounter, with rituals and practices designed to draw people into a place where they can be open to God. The fundamental goal of the service is to experience God through the Spirit (Anderson, 2004, pp. 187–98; Albrecht, 1996, pp. 107–25). For many in these traditions, a service without a time of sung worship or focused listening to God may struggle to be considered an experience of worship, yet celebrating communion only once a month is not unusual.

A sacramental understanding of church, typified in the Roman Catholic Church or Anglo-Catholic traditions of the Church of England, would emphasize Eucharist and baptism over and above Scripture, community and a dependence on the Spirit. Sacraments are the central element of church. The other elements either flow from them or feed into them. For instance, the sacraments mediate the fellowship of life with God. The church as a communion can only be understood through the communal sharing of the mass. The Catholic systematic theologian Michael Fahey writes that the sacraments are 'gospel words expressed in such a way that the words are intensified by ritual gesture' (1992, p. 38). In the church, Scripture is still present, as is the Spirit, but it is clear from Fahey's later words that he sees sacraments as the defining constituent of the church: 'the church when celebrating any sacrament, but especially at the memorial of the Lord's Supper, the Eucharist, achieves an intensity of its being that is quite central to its self-identity' (1992, p. 38). A service without the Eucharist would usually not be considered complete. In the Anglican Church the parish communion movement in the early twentieth century emerged from the Anglo-Catholic wing of the denomination to encourage a weekly celebration of the Eucharist at a church's main service on Sundays.

Martin Luther was committed to sacraments but central to his theology was the idea that salvation is accessed by faith alone, through grace alone. He had a high emphasis on Scripture: 'The church is the gathering of all believers, in which the gospel is purely preached and the holy sacraments are properly administered' (Augsburg Confession, 7:1) – church membership is accessed through faith and received through responding to the proclamation of Scripture. The sacraments are there to strengthen faith. His ideas have permeated protestant theology and are influential in many denominations.

These are just three examples out of many that demonstrate the sheer range of approaches that can be taken by different traditions, which affect the shape of church. Each would have something different to say about church structure and hierarchy too, despite their all having the common foundations of Scripture, sacraments, community and dependence on the Spirit.

Putting Michael Moynagh's four criteria – that a new contextual church must be missional, contextual, formational and ecclesial (outlined in Chapter 1; Moynagh, 2012, p. xiv) – alongside the four aspects mentioned above from different traditions, I could argue that for a church to be both an authentic fresh expression and authentically church, it would need the ingredients of sacrament, fellowship, Scripture, Spirit, mission, disciple-making and contextualization. The 2012 report *Fresh*

Expressions in the Mission of the Church, written to add to the theology and answer critiques of *Mission-Shaped Church*, produced a list that encompasses all of these aspects but adds three more elements: structure; hierarchy; attention to the historical church. The writers argue that church is a community:

- where people are called by God to be committed disciples of Jesus Christ and to live out their discipleship in the world;
- that regularly assembles for Christian worship and is then sent out into the world to engage in mission and service;
- in which the gospel is proclaimed in ways appropriate to the lives of its members;
- in which the Scriptures are regularly preached and taught;
- in which baptism is conferred in appropriate circumstances as a rite of initiation into the Church;
- that celebrates the Lord's Supper;
- where pastoral responsibility and presidency at the Lord's Supper is exercised by the appropriate authorized ministry;
- that is united to others through mutual commitment; spiritual communion; structures of governance, oversight and communion; an authorized ministry in common. (2012, p. 181)

The report goes on to say that if a Christian community lacks even one of these elements, then it is not a church:

> It would be incorrect to describe such a community as 'a form of church' or 'a church for the people involved'. This would be to replace an objective definition with a subjective definition that sells short the gospel and thus fails those whom it is intended to benefit. (p. 181)

This would imply that, according to this report, the above list of eight marks are all essential qualities for a fresh expression to be a church. Yet another approach, similar to many of the elements above, comes from the Chicago–Lambeth Quadrilateral, a four-point articulation of Anglican identity adopted in the late nineteenth century, of Scripture, creed, sacraments and episcopal ministry.[13]

My point here is that many have attempted to distil the essence of church into a set of guidelines, activities or practices. Some of these amount to broadly similar points, and any one of these lists can be a helpful way to think about church. However, while I affirm the importance of each of the practices on the lists, they can come across as one-dimensional and can fail to capture the essence, feeling and relationships involved in the church, as well as the stage of that church community's development. These are broad and generalizable lists, so there is also no mention of the contexts that lead to those practices taking shape, therefore what these practices should look like. This is the key problem when it comes to defining church by practices: Christians struggle to agree on what these practices should look like. The danger is that a list such as this is read through preconceived notions of church tradition, so that the value of certain practices can fail to be appreciated by those from another tradition.

To give an example of how differing approaches may be received, in Pete Ward's edited volume *Mass Culture*, Mike Riddell describes an event he was involved in at the alternative worship church Parallel Universe in New Zealand (Riddell, 1999, pp. 95–115). The theme for the evening was Jesus' feeding of the 5,000, which has clear eucharistic overtones. Parallel Universe re-enacted this story using beer and pies; the leader lifted the pie and the can of beer towards heaven and used the words of initiation: 'God, me old mate, we'll be snorkelling in the sewage pond if you don't help us out. We ain't got much, but what we've got we give to you' (p. 97). The pie was then broken, the can opened and passed around. This experiment was appreciated on the night and appeared to be contextually appropriate to the people attending. However, a traditionalist reading this account might be scandalized and struggle to see how this can possibly be authentic communion, due to the lack of bread, wine and authorized words of institution (although Riddell does go on to talk about how important it is that creativity is rooted firmly in tradition). Similarly, a free-church evangelical might attend a certain liberal-catholic mass and be dismayed at the shortness of the homily, lack of Bibles in the pews, overuse of ritual or lack of depth in teaching the Scriptures. Given this, an over-reliance on defining church by what goes on will always lead to disagreements over what is and isn't appropriate. This is why, in the final three chapters of this book, while I do not dismiss these practices as being unimportant, I do argue for a cross-shaped approach that centres the work of the church on the work of Christ, and takes the starting point of looking for Christ's work in the practices and ministries of the church. In this way, cross-centredness can be applied equally into many different traditions and is less concerned with the shape of the practices that may be encountered.

Steven Croft, current Bishop of Oxford, in his earlier role as leader of the Fresh Expressions organization, wrote of 'distilled ecclesiologies' that uncover the essence of what it means to be church, without defining the practices within them too rigidly (2008b, pp. 188–9). This way of thinking refers to broad categories that any church would adhere to, but within each there could be plenty of variation and creativity. The description of the post-Pentecost church in Acts 2 would be an example, gathered around Scripture, teaching, breaking of bread, fellowship and prayer. Although the Acts 2 church did things in a particular way, relevant to their context, there is no suggestion from Croft that their practices need to be copied precisely. He also mentions another distilled ecclesiology, which emerges from the Nicene Creed – the concepts of one, holy, catholic and apostolic (Croft, 2008b, p. 189). These are promoted by *Mission-Shaped Church*, p. 99) and used in Fresh Expressions training.

Another distilled ecclesiology that could be applied is in the three directions of the triangle *up*, *in* and *out* described in Mike Breen and Walt Kallestad's 'Life Shapes' model (2005, pp. 82–104). This is outlined in their book *The Passionate Church* and also mentioned in *Mission-Shaped Church*, which adds the additional direction, *of* (p. 99).[14] The four directions indicate *up* towards God in worship and discipleship, *in* towards each other in community and fellowship, *out* to the world in mission, and being *of* the wider and inherited Church, a framework that has the advantage of being focused on relationships rather than structures or practices. Breen and

Kallestad argue that all churches, indeed all ministries of the church, should have the three directions to them to a greater or lesser degree.

There is clearly much more to be said on the specifics within distilled ecclesiologies, but each can give a start and offers a way into investigating the basis of what it means to be church. Each distilled ecclesiology gives a theological foundation that allows the fresh expression, indeed any church, to be evaluated in a less prescriptive and concrete manner than simply looking at practices. The moves of God cannot be kept in neat categories, as the early Church discovered throughout the book of Acts. For example, the scattering of believers due to persecution forced them to settle away from Jerusalem and re-imagine church for their new contexts (Acts 7–9). This also opened up the faith to a new set of people, namely Samaritans and God-fearing Gentiles. Similarly, Peter's call to visit Cornelius forced him to redefine his concept of who the church is for, and paved the way for the mission to the Gentiles (Acts 10). Distilled ecclesiologies give space for contextualization while remaining faithful to central aspects of what it means to be church.

Our way forward

With so many examples and approaches to choose from, how would we structure our worship and what would we do during our time together? It would have been easy to go down the Messy Church route. This was something we were considering due to the high number of primary and pre-school children on the estate. Messy Church offers a recognizable branding with off-the-peg resources, which makes it possible even for small churches with limited resources to launch a fresh expression for families and children.[15] While it is true that in some cases Messy Churches have become simply a children's ministry of a church rather than a church congregation in themselves, many offer an alternative family-friendly approach to worship that draws in those who would otherwise not come. Whether they are considered to be church rather than a ministry of a church comes down to whether they are seen as congregations to develop and disciple in themselves, which share all aspects of life and faith together, rather than as a stepping stone to 'proper church' on Sunday mornings.[16] Having said this, even in such cases the resources and branding available has given many congregations a clear path to engage non-churchgoing parents and children.

After serious consideration of Messy Church we looked at the size and life-stage of our core team (small in number and with very young children), and wondered whether we had the resources between us to pull it off successfully. We also did not have access to a large meeting space on our housing development. In hindsight, perhaps we could have managed a scaled-down version starting in a home, but we hadn't thought about that at the time. Another important factor was also in play. While we were deliberating, a nearby Baptist church had announced that they were going to start Messy Church in the school on their neighbouring development. They had a large team from an established congregation to support them. The obvious solution was to partner with them in leading and supporting theirs. With their blessing we were able to join residents from our development in that Messy Church and build relationships with them while there.

But it was still important to have a gathering for our housing development, to draw together our core team and offer a worshipping focus to the many activities our church was already undertaking. I was drawn towards the café-church approach, as it was informal, gave plenty of space for relationships to develop and allowed a lot of flexibility in content.

Learning from others

As I was considering these questions, the latest issue of *Encounters on the Edge* dropped through my door. This was a quarterly publication, now discontinued, from the Church Army about fresh expressions and church planting.[17] The subject of this issue was an in-depth study of River Community Church, which served new-build developments on the outskirts of Telford, Shropshire (Lings, 2011a). As I read, I remembered that I had met the minister, Revd Steve Kelly, and his wife Maggie before at a conference the previous year, when we had swapped contact details. So I called him up and arranged to visit their monthly Sunday café church, which took place in a local village hall.

When we arrived half an hour early, the room was already set up ready for their 3.30 p.m. start. There were five little clusters of chairs gathered around tables. On each table were some leaflets, a plate of sweets and a menu card detailing what was going to happen throughout the afternoon. The theme was written in bold on the front of the menu: 'We're in a Battle'. At the back of the room was a welcome table with information, newsletters and books, and another table serving coffee and tea. By the side wall of the hall, tables were set out with craft materials, which would be used later in the service for prayer. The band was situated at the front corner of the hall and next to them was an area cordoned off with school benches. Behind the benches was a candle, a small cross with the name 'Jesus' written on it, and a big screen for projection.

As we came in, coffee was available and people were chatting. Noticing that we were new, some made a point of coming over to welcome us. One lady who introduced herself as the families worker spotted that we had a toddler. She was giving the talk that day and wanted to warn us that she was using the battle clips from the film *The Chronicles of Narnia*, which could be a little bit scary for younger children. By the time the service started, there were about 25 people including children, who ranged in age from 5 to 13.

Steve introduced the service and welcomed everyone before we sang a song, and engaged in an ice-breaker game on the theme of 'battles'. This was followed by the first clip from the film. After another song, in which the children were encouraged to join in on small drums, a few verses from the Bible were read by a child. Then the children's worker took the floor for the 25-minute teaching slot. The talk was punctuated with video clips and illustrations and finished with some personal testimony. The take-home point: We're in a battle but God is with us in it, alongside. Overall this was a decent talk, but could have been complemented by more time to discuss the nature of the battles we are facing.

Next the two craft activities that had been laid out in advance were needed for the prayer time. For the first, each person was invited to write someone's name on a paper cut-out of a hand and then place their hand over it saying a prayer. The second involved writing a prayer on some cross-shaped paper and putting it at the front of the hall at the foot of the cross. People were also welcome to pray silently in place or with others around their table if they preferred, while the band played soft music. The theme of the prayers was for those who are struggling or 'in a battle'. The prayer time concluded with an invitation for people to gather around one of the congregants who had been struggling. Another song brought the service to a close.

Given that the vast majority of our core team had children under the age of four, we were particularly interested in how our toddler would cope with the format. Ours was the only pre-schooler in the service, and he remained fairly engaged until about halfway through the talk. He enjoyed the interaction, the drum, the music and the first video clip. After that he began to lose interest, so my wife took him outside the room to run around, coming back in for the prayer crafts after the talk had finished. Steve admitted later that while they did have a number of families with children, they did not at that time have any pre-schoolers attending the service, so it was not created with this age-group in mind.

Afterwards there was plenty of time to chat with others over more coffee, tea, cakes and chocolates. No one seemed in a desperate hurry to leave, and we could tell this was an important time of fellowship for them. Again people were friendly. Some games had been provided for the children in a corner. It was not until just after 5 p.m. that the chairs began to be cleared away.

Steve and Maggie then very graciously offered to debrief us after the service in a nearby pizza restaurant. Sharing the history of the church, Steve put their current practices in a broader context. First, he said that the monthly service was set up about three years ago for seekers, emerging from a Christmas activity, which was the first public event they did. From there they found

that a number of unchurched people in the housing development wanted to keep meeting and discovering faith together, so
the café church was born. When they first began there would
have been more interaction around tables and they wouldn't
have started with sung worship. Any songs sung would have
been performed from the front, with the expectation that people
would only join in if they wanted to. Also, the topics discussed
would have been lighter and more suitable for those early in
their Christian journey. Now, in addition to the café church,
they ran a contemporary-worship service on two of the other
Sundays each month. On one Sunday per month there was no
service. The rationale for this was not only resourcing but to
enable church members who lived far from family to feel they
could be away visiting them fairly regularly without having to
miss church. The interactive café-church style was intended as
a way for the whole church family to learn together in various
ways and at different levels at the same time. The format also
allowed them to approach the theme of the service from a number of different angles.

After a couple of years, congregation numbers started to plateau. As fewer new people came through the door, Steve and
Maggie decided to concentrate on the people they had, taking
them deeper in faith. At the same time, Steve was in the process
of helping the congregation to discern ways of reaching new
people. They had begun to realize that the church was mas-
sively dependent on them as a couple and this was preventing
them moving forward, so Steve put steps in place to empower
the congregation to take more of a lead. New leaders needed
to emerge in order to free up Steve and Maggie and enable the
church as a whole to reach out further. It was clear that this
was a congregation that had been on a journey starting with
interested seekers who were now developing in discipleship
and leadership.

What shape would our gatherings take?

As we started to think about gathering together, we had to
discern who our gathering was for and what we would do

when we met. There were certainly similarities between our context and that of River Community Church, as well as significant differences. Although the motivation for starting to gather together had come from the particular needs of the core team, we felt that if we were going to meet together then we should strive to have something that was suitable for current non-churchgoers to drop into easily. At this stage in our development there were 15 of us, counting the core team and their children. We also knew another three or four families and fringe Christians who might come along to worship. Meeting for worship would form a stronger common identity as we started receiving deeper teaching together. At that time it was often only those who did not work who most regularly met together during the week. A gathering at another time of the week would enable those who work to participate more fully. There was also the possibility that one or two more Christians who had moved into the area might hear about what we were doing and start worshipping with us too. We wanted our gathering to be open to all but would strive to help all move forward with their faith. We would not neglect the other aspects of our work, which were doing well at reaching out to the development. However, a gathering for worship would give us a focus and a point of entry where people who were not free in the week could find us if they wanted. It would also very quickly provide an answer to the regularly asked question: 'So where do you meet?' We felt ready, but what should our worship look like? These questions were by no means unique to us. Many churches and pioneering initiatives find, as they reach out to new contexts, that they need to rethink their practice of church, and in particular what happens when they gather together.

Having revisited the exercise we had done together as a core team in our initial meetings to identify the values we thought were important to us, we began to make progress. For our main gatherings we wanted to think of a format that would reflect these values and be appropriate to the context. A simple structure of worship, discussion, talk, prayer and response would suffice. The interactive format with plenty of discussion would ensure we would reflect our values of being fun and interesting. The talks would be scripturally based, ensuring we stayed Bible-centred – another of our values. The discussion would help build relationships and community within the group, and this value would be reinforced by making a sandwich tea an integral part of the gathering. All would be done within a context of welcome and hospitality. We settled on a format that embraced all of these concerns.

In order to help create a hospitable feel (and for lack of another suitable venue), we decided to hold the first service in our house. We had already built relationships with most of the people we were expecting to come, many of whom had visited our home before, so the house had the advantage of being both known to them and comfortable.

After debating the merits and drawbacks of trying to make the service all-age, we concluded, initially at least, that having separate children's activities would enable them to receive age-appropriate content while the adults could engage in a way that is not always possible with toddlers in the room. Of course, this decision meant that we needed to find people who might lead the activities for pre-schoolers, but we were confident that this would be possible. The choice of Sunday at 4 p.m. arose from the preferences of the group and the research conducted (described in Chapter 1), which I had held in the local Indian restaurant. This enabled those with unbelieving partners to feel that they didn't have to choose between church and family time on Sunday mornings. Children could still get to Sunday-morning sports activities should they desire, and it would be perfectly possible to go away to visit family for the weekend and get back in time for the gathering.

The initial meeting was a bit of a squeeze. Although our house was one of the biggest on the development, the living room could only sit seven or eight people comfortably. We squashed in a few more dining chairs so that there was just about room for the 11 adults and 7 children who came. We had publicized the gathering through the groups we were already running, and our core team had been active in inviting their friends. In the recent past three couples, residents of the development, had approached me asking to have their child baptized. I had taken them through baptism preparation as a group – to build relationships between them – and had baptized their children in other local churches. One of these couples came to the first gathering and the other two came the following month. Of the three couples, two would become regular attenders at the monthly gatherings. Another couple who came were from a different part of Northampton. They had been along to our baby signing group (see Chapter 2), invited because they were friends with a core team member who lived on our street. They came with their daughter and remained regulars throughout my time in Northampton, growing in faith along the way.

The children would be in with the adults for the first 10–15 minutes, as I introduced the theme and we sang a song together that most of the children were familiar with. The kids were then taken to our family living room – a converted bedroom – on the second floor, where they would do a craft and hear some stories. The rest of the adults then settled into the 45-minute slot focused on our theme for the day (God's grace), through a mixture of upfront input, discussion and video clips. Finally we had a worship activity (which didn't involve singing), and a prayer and response time. Apart from the children's song at the beginning, we limited communal singing until the congregation had become better acquainted with one another and started to journey in their faith a little. I also thought singing together while sitting around in our front room might feel weird to non-Christians: apart from at football matches or pub singalongs, there aren't many occasions in British culture when adults sing together. I regard communal singing as one of the most countercultural aspects of church – even though I happen to like it.

Following the planned activities we always stayed and ate together. For ease of planning and hosting we had ordered pre-prepared sandwich platters from the local supermarket, which we supplemented with drinks and desserts. We had made it clear from the outset that our time of eating together was as important as the 'service' itself. It was to be the time when we shared the joys and struggles of our lives, grew together and built deep friendships. We were engaging in *koinonia*. Without this time I wonder whether our fledgling community would have gelled in the same way. It had a practical dimension to it as well: as each of us had small children, we could now go home and easily get them bathed and to bed, knowing they and we had already eaten.

After that first meeting, as we were tidying up, Sarah and I were elated. It came four weeks after the birth of our second child, so this was a wonderful time of blessing in our lives. I was very happy that the fringe Christians came and that one particular couple not only came but were so enthusiastic about it that they were eager to come back the next time. There was also encouragement from some unchurched friends I had invited but who had not replied. They texted halfway through to say they were intending to come but had become stuck in traffic returning from a day out. The level of interaction during the discussion, icebreaker and prayer time was promising too for the growing of our community. People shared honest heart-felt prayers. Almost all stayed for the food afterwards, and I think this time helped relationships to deepen, especially given that this was our first gathering and where some were meeting others for the first time. One unchurched husband who hadn't been at the service joined us for the meal afterwards.

There were still things to learn. I spoke about the message of grace based on the story of the woman caught in adultery in John 8, in which Jesus saves her from a stoning. Although I felt that most people were engaged during the input and dis-cussion time, I wondered if the topic was a bit too heavy for the unchurched people in the first session.

The following month we did it again. This time there were 12 adults and 7 children attending. Five of the adults were different adults – most of those who had not returned from the previous month had family commitments that weekend – and six were unchurched. We had one husband who didn't want to come to the service but was happy to help the children's leader with their session. This left us in such a place that if all the adults came there at one time, there would be nearly 20. Clearly our living room was going to get squashed! If we were going to progress we would have to start meeting somewhere else. With the planned community centre for the development still not underway, this would unfortunately mean meeting in a location away from the estate. At that time we thought this would only be a temporary solution for a year to 18 months. We were not to know then that construction of the community centre would only begin after we had left Berrywood.

Applying the marks of church

Although this was not something we did at the time, applying Steve Croft's concept of distilled ecclesiologies shows that we had taken steps towards being church. While the transition from being a fledgling group of Christians meeting together for mutual support into becoming church was not straightforward, these lenses help us to see that the essential qualities of church were becoming present. The credal statement of *one*, *holy*, *catholic* and *apostolic*, mentioned in *Mission-Shaped Church*, was beginning to hold (pp. 96–100). We were *one* in that we were united to the universal Church. Our funding and basis was Anglican but our core team had welcomed Catholics and Evangelicals alike. We were becoming *holy* as we brought our lives together to grow in faith and sought to reach outwards in mission. We were *catholic* in the diversity of backgrounds in our group and the sense that everyone was welcome, although in this regard I admit that we were all from the same life-stage. As the church developed, a few people of other ethnicities joined us too. And we were *apostolic* in that we were continuing the actions of the early Church, meeting in small groups, teaching from Scripture, sharing our lives.

Applying the four-directional distilled ecclesiology to our situation would work too. We had started the *up* dimension in worshipping together; this was simply an extension of what we had already begun in meeting as a core team for Bible study and prayer. We had begun with the *in* and *out* dimensions, in creating community and being at work in the wider community. We had begun to form a close and supportive central group who were both active in looking outward and welcoming others in.

The *of* dimension was present too, as we were commissioned by the Church of England and were committed to working together with other local churches who had a similar vision, particularly Forefront, the Baptist/New Frontiers church who met in the primary school on our development on Sundays, and the Baptist Church in a nearby village who were pioneering on the neighbouring new-build estate of Upton.

***

With these definitions we could be considered to be church. However, they only give a start to our understanding of what is church. The question of 'What is success?' can also begin with such a framework, although in both cases the distilled ecclesiologies need to be fleshed out with a deeper underlying theology. In the next chapter I will investigate and analyse the different theological bases that other fresh expressions practitioners and thinkers have used as a starting point in determining questions of ecclesiology.

Notes

1 See www.tubestation.org.

2 See Knit and Natter: www.community.sharetheguide.org/stories /knitandnatter; accessed 13 Nov. 2017. There is also a fascinating analysis of what makes Knit and Natter 'church' in Christine Dutton's article, *Unpicking Knit and Natter* (2014).

3 'Goth Church, Coventry': www.community.sharetheguide.org /stories/gothchurchcoventry; accessed 13 Nov. 2017.

4 'The Lord is Here', ch. 3 on *Expressions: The DVD 2 – Changing Church in Every Place* (London: Church House Publishing, 2007).

5 See www.northumbriacommunity.org.

6 Their current structure of groups can be viewed at www.moot .uk.net.

7 See ch. 2, 'Legacy XS', on *Expressions: The DVD 1 – Stories of Church for our Changing Culture* (Fresh Expressions, 2006).

8 'See ch. 1, 'Taste and See', on *Expressions: The DVD 1*.

9 'Hartcliffe and Withywood Lighthouse': www.community.sharetheguide.org/stories/lighthouse; accessed 13 Nov. 2017.

10 For more information, see the Fresh Expressions writeup, 'Exeter Network Church': www.community.sharetheguide.org/stories/exeter networkchurch; accessed 13 Nov. 2017, or their own website: www .enc.uk.net.

11 Their website can be found at: http://cnc.church.

12 See 'Midweeker', St Jude's: www.judes.org.uk/about/services /midweeker; accessed 4 July 2016.

13 'The Chicago–Lambeth Quadrilateral: 1888', Anglicans Online: http://anglicansonline.org/basics/Chicago_Lambeth.html; accessed 6 July 2016.

14 *Up, in* and *out* was originally envisaged as three overlapping circles of worship, community and mission by Robert Warren, in *Being Human, Being Church* (1995, p. 89).

15 For example, Messy Church at All Saints, Wheatley Hill in Durham Diocese, was begun by a small elderly congregation during an interregnum (story related to me by the vicar).

16 For a more detailed discussion around whether Messy Churches can be considered church in themselves, see Dalpra (2013, pp. 12–30) and Hollinghurst (2013, pp. 31–47).

17 The whole set of back issues can be downloaded free from: www .churcharmy.org/Groups/244969/Church_Army/Church_Army/Our _work/Research/Encounters_on_the/Encounters_on_the.aspx; accessed 20 Sept. 2017.

4

Does theology matter?

At Berrywood Church our starting point was to try and build community on the housing development. In many ways we were succeeding. Two of the regulars in our Monday Night Football lived two doors away from each other but had never met until they both started coming along to our group. They were both friendly and interesting people with young families, yet because of the lack of community activities and groups on the development up to that point, they had never had the opportunity to get to know each another. The act of playing together once a week and having a drink in the pub afterwards provided a natural environment for them to become friends. I pondered this with satisfaction a few months later as we sat together in one of their back gardens enjoying a barbecue. A degree of local community was being formed.

But 'community' is one of those words that has become over-used. It can describe a geographical area, regardless of whether people know each other or not. It can indicate those who gather around a shared identity or common cause (such as the Goth or LGBTI communities), even if those who belong are spread over a wide geographical area and have never physically met. Or it can denote a group of people who share their lives with one another in close relationship, either living geographically near each other or through, for example, social media. When it came to creating community in St Crispin's, I was thinking of the word in a couple of ways. I wanted people who lived on the development to know each other and be involved in their neighbours' lives, so that this estate was not a community of strangers. When neighbours know one another in such a way it can create safe environments, combatting isolation and loneliness. Out of this geographical community I also wanted to create a more focused community based on a shared desire to explore God together. This community would journey together as they grew in faith.

Most writers on new contextual churches regard the joining or creation of communities as central to the pioneering of a new form of church. The process starts with listening. For example, Dave Male, in *How to Pioneer*, gives several examples of Christian communities that have formed through intentional relationship-building (2016, pp. 54–60). It would therefore be natural to take the biblical notion arising from the Greek word *koinonia*, often translated as 'fellowship', as a starting point for thinking about new contextual churches. In fact this is where the joint Anglican–Methodist report *Fresh Expressions in the Mission of the Church* begins in developing the theology for new ecclesial communities. Going through the practices of the church in the book of Acts, the report finds that the *koinonia* on show in the early Church emphasizes close community, communion, attention to the apostles' teaching, the breaking of bread and prayer (2012, pp. 61–84).

The biblical notion of *koinonia* denotes deep and rich fellowship, far deeper than the surface relationships that form from simply hanging out at 'fellowship time' over a coffee after a church service. In the description of the first believers gathering together after Pentecost, the church is portrayed as being very close, sharing everything, meeting regularly in homes as well as engaging in teaching, prayer and eating together (Acts 2.42–48). In other places *koinonia* describes a state of being joined together, through suffering and close support, to one another and to the Father, Son and Spirit (Gal. 2.9; Phil. 3.10; 1 John 1.3). *Koinonia* could then be described as a sharing of life together and a sharing of God together. With this in mind there is a definite need for close *koinonia* in any new ecclesial community. However, it must be stressed that community-based fellowship in a neighbourhood or network cannot be called *koinonia* without a God aspect to it. *Koinonia* does not just appear out of neighbourhood relations without intentionality, but points of community within a neighbourhood may be a starting point for *koinonia*.

This was evident in Berrywood. I have already described the relationships formed in the pub after our weekly Monday Night Football sessions, with conversations covering a wide range of subjects, from celebrity exploits to serious religious and political matters. From this group came the opportunity for some research with three of the men which formed part of my listening phase of the project, discussing questions of church and faith (described in Chapter 1). This research evening morphed into the regular Curry and Questions group, where we discussed life and faith in more depth. *Koinonia* was developing. Likewise, some of the parents involved in our initial baby signing sessions found an easy transition into the Bible and Bubbles mornings, where members began to share their life and faith closely together. These two examples show how community-building activities can lead to a growing sense of *koinonia* in a group.

This idea of *koinonia* can be seen to be right at the heart of what pioneers should be aiming for in beginning their work. They strive to create an ecclesial community that is:

> not church in the sense of a building with a gathered community and a weekly God-slot with its predictable diet of liturgy and worship, teaching and fellowship and, of course, the offertory. But church in the sense of a Christian community aware of the presence of God, seeking to follow the way of Christ and open to the transforming power of the Holy Spirit wherever [he] happens to be in the world. (Shier-Jones, 2009, p. 7)

From this we can see that close fellowship is there, but it is framed within ideas of the work of Christ, Spirit-led mission and the transformative power of the Father articulated in a Trinitarian manner. Many writers take one of these as their theological starting point for thinking about fresh expressions, with the idea of *koinonia* emanating from that. At the time, our starting point of *koinonia* was pragmatic rather than theological. But does the theological starting point of a pioneering ministry matter? How might it affect the shape or practices of the resulting ecclesial community? In the remainder of this chapter I will examine how the Trinity, mission and other theological doctrines have been used to conceptualize new contextual churches and fresh expressions, and will discuss how these affect our ideas of church.

Trinity

One of the first writers to engage with the doctrine of the Trinity in the context of fresh expressions of church was Ian Mobsby, the former leader of the New Monastic community Moot, based in the City of London.[1] They aim to meet the needs of those in and near the City who are searching for meaning and grounding in the midst of their secular and capitalist environment. Their Sunday services use a variety of traditional liturgies, including Taizé, contemplative services, Eucharist and agape meals. Throughout the week they offer a rhythm of contemplative prayer alongside groups that practise yoga and meditation and who meet for discussion. They also run a café and host occasional events such as poetry evenings. All their events and services are open to anyone to attend, but they do have different levels of membership, which reflect the degree of commitment to the rhythm of life and pattern of prayer of the member.

Mobsby sees the formation of *koinonia* as central in a church community, and therefore indicates that building community can be a fruitful place to start in establishing fresh expressions. For him the notion of *koinonia* is rooted in the doctrine of the Trinity. In the first of his books, *Emerging and Fresh Expressions of Church*, he argues that as the church should be seen as a reflection of the character of God, the Trinity is a useful approach to thinking about fresh expressions, giving a dimension of close community that springs from the character of God (2007, pp. 51ff.). He fleshes out his Trinitarian theology in two subsequent books, *The Becoming of G_d* (2008) and its revised and expanded version, *God Unknown*

(2012). Although he bases his theology on a particular idea of the social Trinity that is not universally accepted by systematic theologians (briefly examined below), I include it here, as it helpfully connects the life of God to the life and rhythms of worshippers.

Social Trinitarianism focuses on the relationships between the persons of the Trinity rather than the essence or nature of each person. The idea of *perichoresis*, first used in the sixth century by a writer usually now referred to as Pseudo-Cyril, indicates a movement of the persons of the Trinity in and around each other. The South American liberation theologian Leonardo Boff describes it as follows: 'perichoresis means one Person's action of involvement with the other two. Each divine Person permeates the other and allows itself to be permeated by that person' (2000, p. 14). From this idea, and relying on a renewal of interest in the Trinity in the twentieth century from such luminaries as Karl Barth and Karl Rahner, theologians such as Boff, John Zizioulas (1985) and Paul Fiddes (2000) have developed the theology of the social Trinity further in the last 40 years. *Perichoresis* became likened to a 'divine dance' emphasizing the patterns of the dance of relationships within the Trinity, rather than the persons of it, implying a God who moves and effects change through the participation in him (Fiddes, 2000, pp. 71–4). This idea of God was then mapped on to the church to create a model of the Church as a network of personal relationships.[2]

Mobsby is drawing on one of the five models of the church of the Catholic theologian Cardinal Avery Dulles: the church as a 'mystical communion'. Dulles intended this to sit alongside and overlapping the other models of church: as institution, sacrament, herald and servant (Dulles, 1974). It is notable that Mobsby has chosen only to draw on one of the models in his theology. Church as a mystical communion is an interpersonal fellowship, reflecting the body of Christ and the indwelling of Christ in the believer. Dulles writes that: 'The goal of the Church . . . is a spiritual or supernatural one. The Church aims to lead men into communion with the divine' (1974, p. 58). To continue Mobsby's argument, applying this model to new forms of church, believers are then able to connect with the rhythms of the living God as he draws them to him, and these rhythms become evident in believers' relationships with him and with one another. Because God is to be experienced, church is participatory. God is 'characterised by unity in diversity, perfect love, justice and interdependency' (Mobsby, 2008, p. 28). Worship should therefore be about going deeper into the Trinitarian God through the Spirit, participating in him as Creator (Father), Redeemer (Son) and Sustainer (Spirit), and participating with all creation where God is within and sustains all things (2008, p. 40).

Worship of the Trinitarian God therefore affects how Christians live. The Trinitarian relationships are characterized by a 'pouring out' or 'self-giving' of one into the other, which Mobsby calls *kenosis* (2008, p. 49). This is the same term used by Paul speaking of Jesus in Philippians, who 'did not consider equality with God something to be used to his own advantage; rather, he made himself nothing by taking the very nature of a servant' in becoming human (Phil. 2.6–7). As the Creator pours out love into the Redeemer and Sustainer, together they pour out love into the world. Mobsby claims that Christian communities who are self-giving in their engagement with the world model the relationships of the Trinity and are participating in those relationships: 'we share in God's nature and help bring all things back into relationship with him' (2008, p. 49). So church is about participating in the Trinitarian relationships of God, which includes how God relates to the world.

As church is about engaging with the *perichoresis* of God, marks of the church, such as sacraments, Scripture and laws, are there to enable people to participate in this mystical communion with God by grace. In the Eucharist, God is made present through the sacrament to those present. Through it they are able to participate 'through the Spirit in the Son's communion with the Father' (Mobsby, 2008, p. 41), and therefore have *koinonia* with one another. As the Eucharist ends, worshippers are sent out into the world to, as the Anglican liturgy states, 'love and serve the Lord' and therefore participate in God's action in the world.

The advantages of thinking about church in this way are that it emphasizes *koinonia*-fellowship within the church and allows people to experience God. It therefore lends itself to new monastic thinking such as that of Moot and Mobsby. As the community is not only participating with each other but participating in the life of God, theoretically this means that the church will be able to respond quickly to contextual change as they follow his lead in the world.

I agree that emphasizing fellowship is vital. Close fellowship is increasingly hard to detect in our fragmenting society. Even in churches, sometimes only loose or superficial community is present rather than close *koinonia*. How often can it be claimed that congregations are sharing all of life's joys and sorrows together? In the wider community I have already mentioned how, in my context, two men who lived two doors away from each other had never met until we started our community football group. Their lives were enhanced once they, and their families, got to know one another, even though at that point they were not yet sharing God together. Another example is Jenny, the young mum who after moving to the estate with her husband was feeling quite isolated for many months. She began to participate in some of our community activities, which eventually led to a discovery of her faith. Her story is told in detail in the final chapter of this book. I would say these examples of building community in the neighbourhood offer a way into *koinonia* rather than being *koinonia* in themselves. However, it is possible to argue, rather tenuously, from this form of Trinitarian thinking that developing interdependency within communities can be seen as enabling people to participate in the relationships of the Trinity, whether God is acknowledged or not.[3]

There is much to commend the Trinity as a theological starting point. Encouraging close communion with God and with one another are surely things that churches should be striving for. However, there are some dangers to this approach. First, in starting with the social Trinity, other important aspects of fresh expressions thinking, such as mission, become add-ons to the life of the church community. Mobsby remarks: 'Mission becomes the activities that dispose people to an interior experience of belonging and eventual union with God effected by grace' (2008, p. 71). Mission as the outworking of *koinonia* in this Trinitarian model of church could easily be seen as a second thought. At best it can leave church with a purely attractional approach to mission, as it is *koinonia* that draws people into God and enables them to participate in him. This is evident in the stated rhythm of life of the Moot community Mobsby used to lead, where mission can be seen as implicit rather than explicit (2008, pp. 78–9). Moot's values include presence, acceptance, creativity, balance, accountability and hospitality. The value of *koinonia* is clearly evident. Mission is present in this rhythm of life but is not in the forefront of it. It would be possible to read Moot's rhythm-of-life statement alone without gaining an understanding of how outreach in their context occurs. Of course, a quick look at their current practices overcomes this concern, showing that their values of hospitality and creativity are played out in mission as they offer artistic events, yoga and meditation that are open to the wider public, and as they invite people into their recently opened coffee shop in the church building. These appear to be contextual, given the part of London in which they are located, and may well work within a fast-changing networked community, but in more settled geographical communities, such as new-build developments, using the social Trinity as a starting point to conceptualizing church may result in an attractional church model, one that often already exists and for many demographics is not effective, which sees mission as an added extra.

Second, this approach suffers from some fundamental theological problems too. Mobsby's argument relies on our having an understanding of how the persons of the Trinity relate to one another. Responding to proponents of social Trinitarianism, the Catholic systematic theologian Karen Kilby asks whether we can actually know what is going on within the Godhead. Kilby calls this a problem of projection (2000, pp. 432–45). Certain attributes are borrowed from human experience and projected on to the inner life of God to overcome our difficulty in thinking about God. Hence we start to talk about relationships, divine dances and so on. These same attributes are then reflected back to the world as a source of insight for humanity, becoming a circular argument. Kilby argues that we cannot know the extent to which *perichoresis* affects the inner life of God and we should not therefore use such speculations as a source for organizing the church. This critique could also hold for other theological concepts, particularly *missio Dei*, which I will look at next. If we take anything from this discussion, it is that care needs to be taken when applying theological concepts to human situations, to ensure we are not projecting our own ideas, which may or may not be true, on to God before applying them straight back again. Given these concerns, perhaps the social Trinity is not a good theological foundation for new ecclesial communities.

While we can say that humanity is invited to participate in the relationships of the Trinity through the Son (cf. John 17.20–24), it cannot be argued that humanity can fully participate in the same way as the Son in our present state. Humanity has the promise of final fulfilment, guaranteed through Christ, but this is not yet complete, and we are not yet transformed fully into Christ's likeness (1 Cor. 15.49). Therefore instead of asking 'How does the Trinity relate to human relationships?' it may be better to ask 'How does God as Trinity relate to humanity?' There is a Trinitarian aspect to human community, through the Son by the Spirit, yet it is God who makes the initial move in reaching out to humanity. Starting here can give us more confidence in the nature of the relationship between humanity and God, and thus the nature of our relationships with one another. This movement of redemption and reconciliation, out from God to humanity and drawing back to himself, is Christological and is found in the act of atonement, which will be explored in the next chapter.

Before moving on from the subject of Trinity, it is worth briefly considering the position of another prominent fresh expressions writer, Martyn Atkins, who develops the doctrine in relation to the church but comes to it from a different angle. Where Mobsby's Trinitarianism focuses on community, with mission flowing from that, Atkins emphasizes the missionary nature of God. He states that the Trinitarian nature of God is revealed in God as missionary and evangelist: 'The God of the Christian Scriptures . . . is first to last, a God of mission' (2007, pp. 12–18). The Father creates and calls; the Son redeems and renews; the Spirit emboldens, leads and sends. Mission is a central aspect of the character of each member of the Trinity. This action of God results in a Spirit-filled missionary people in the church, focused on kingdom issues. And this is the first job of the church, not an optional add-on. Also derived from a Trinitarian understanding of God, this approach places mission at the heart of the church. Mission is, in fact, where many writers on the subject begin, although whether it should be seen as the first job of the church is debated. This is what I will examine next.

Mission

The Mission of God, or *missio Dei*, is often used as a foundation and has been given prominence since the publication of *Mission-Shaped Church* (pp. 20, 83). Mission seems like a natural place to start when thinking of new forms of church that are intended for the unchurched. Fresh expressions thinking arose from those who had a desire to reach people not being reached by traditional church. Many new ecclesial communities begin from a desire to see people in a particular culture or community come to know and follow Christ. Indeed, at Berrywood we wanted not only to establish a sense of community on the housing development but also to create opportunities for people to explore faith and encounter Christ. When we started, even though we began by building community, I would have said we were primarily about mission. What effect does this starting point have on the understanding of church?

Because of their missional emphasis, the starting point in thinking about fresh expressions is often going out to 'be where the people are', as opposed to drawing them into a church community; it is missional rather than attractional. However, both fresh expressions and *Mission-Shaped Church* have been criticised on this point, the claim being that this not only affects ideas of mission but also alters the perception of God. Roger Walton has argued that fresh expressions promote a view that God is not active outside the church (Walton, 2008). This critique is based on an inadequate view of the mission of God.

How, then, does the missional activity of God relate to the church? There is little opposition to the idea that the church should be about mission in some form. What is debated is the role mission should have within it – particularly pertinent for fresh expressions, which are often founded from missionary impulses. As Martyn Atkins indicated, *missio Dei* itself derives from the Trinitarian nature of God. The sending of the Son and Spirit by the Father fulfils creation; the Son redeems the world; the Holy Spirit sustains creation and shares in the mission of the Father and Son. The church is empowered by the Spirit and participates in the work. One approach is to argue that mission, which is an overflow of the sending of the Son and the Spirit, is about how God relates to the world and is therefore a second step for God – the first step being the redemptive sending of the Son, and the second the missional and sustaining sending of the Spirit (Flett, 2010, pp. 29–30). Mapping this on to the church, mission could then be legitimately seen as an add-on to the life of the church – a non-essential. A second approach is to argue that mission is central to God's character and could therefore be described as an attribute of God (Holmes, 2006, p. 89). Mission might then be regarded a first step for the church. Neither of these two approaches are ideal as mission is evidently not the entirety of God's character; likewise is it not an optional extra to his being. As mission cannot encompass the totality of God's work, from creation to the cross, mission as a first step for a church may therefore be as unhelpful as thinking about it as an add-on. Michael Moynagh analyses both of these claims and steers a middle way. He prefers to think of mission as an eternal and ever-continuing aspect of God's self-giving to humanity. Mission is not an attribute of God but all of God's attributes are missionary (2014, pp. 80–3; 2012, pp. 124–6). The church should therefore be about mission because the church is about God. It is neither a first nor second step but exists within everything the church may be and do. This expands mission to be much more than simply the evangelization, gathering in, salvation and discipleship of people, to include the entire work of God springing from his sending nature. Therefore the missional activity of the Church is tied to the mission of God but cannot be said to be the entirety of it.

Stuart Murray was one of the founders of the Urban Expressions church-planting movement, which encourages long-term engagement in areas of deprivation. He is passionate about growing new congregations in such areas but is aware that this is just a part of the mission of God. Writing before the Fresh Expressions movement got going, he sums up the entirety of God's purposes:

> God's missionary purposes are cosmic in scope, concerned with the restoration of all things, the establishment of shalom, the renewal of creation and the coming of the kingdom, as well as the redemption of fallen humanity and the building of the church. (1998, p. 31)

Ecclesiality, while essential, will be only part of the missionary activity of pioneering initiatives if they are seeking to join with the mission of God. This combats Walton's critique that fresh expressions suggest that God is not active outside the church. It also brings the discussion into the territory of the whole work of God.

Mission also affects the intention of the church to reproduce, both in the impetus that leads to the new contextual church being formed in the first place, and the intention of that church to continue to seek opportunities to create additional new ecclesial communities. In his most recent book, *Reproducing Churches*, George Lings agrees that mission cannot be seen as the first step for, or indeed the whole identity of the church. However, he argues for the idea of reproduction as an essential quality of the Church, one he claims has mostly been overlooked throughout history, especially during the era of Christendom. God's mission to the world, he suggests, implies among other things that churches should continue to reproduce, not just grow.

In developing his argument he brings together social Trinitarian thinking and the missiological thinking of the *missio Dei*. Usually writers have tended to focus on one or the other, whereas Lings makes a bridge between the two to make a case for contextual church planting. What follows comes with the caveats about social Trinitarianism that I entered above.

As there are characteristics of reproduction within God, in the sending of the Spirit by the Son and the Son by the Father, and in the overflowing of the life of communion within God to the world (*missio Dei*), these characteristics overflow into the being of the Church. Lings writes:

> Connection with the Trinity raises the bar to the level of being or ontology. It begins to look as if God as Trinity, as community-in-mission, themselves reproduce this identity in the being of the Church. Church life is, in turn, communal, relational, giving, creative, and missional. (Lings, 2017, p. 80)

God is in the business of reproducing, but he doesn't reproduce himself. God's reproduction does not result in more gods. It is the qualities and character of God that are reproduced in the Church. Applying this more concretely, Lings emphasizes several qualities that are essential in the Church (2017, pp. 88–90). First, the Church is relational. This would seem to promote a community approach to church planting. Second, when the church reproduces, what is reproduced is church. Therefore church plants and fresh expressions are 'church' from the day they are conceived, even before they have gathered together for worship or gained new disciples. Lings adds: 'the source and the intention are the diagnostic, not the performance' (2017, p. 89). Third, given that God's reproduction does not result in more gods and human reproduction does not give rise to clones, church reproduction does not result in exact replicas of the sending congregation. The DNA is passed on, along with some of the characteristics and identity. Like the persons of the Trinity, where the Son is a person and is God but is distinct from the Father, the new expression of church is 'church' but is distinct from the church that sent it. As the DNA is passed on, the essential qualities of church can be present (such as some of the distilled ecclesiologies mentioned in the previous chapter). The reproducing nature of church carries over too.

Lings' work is useful, as he has located the characteristic of reproduction as an essential mark of the Church. He makes the case for the establishment of new contextual church communities as a matter of course rather than as interesting exceptions, arguing from the nature of God himself, both his missionary characteristics and the nature of the Trinity. However, given that Lings bases this strand of his argument on the internal workings of the Godhead understood as the social Trinity, this aspect of his argument suffers from the same problems of projection that Kilby highlights, detailed above. This does not, however, undermine the rest of his discussion of reproduction, which he bases on creation, the Gospels and the Holy Spirit.

The way to approach the question of mission in the Church is not by starting with mission. If we are to locate the discussion of new contextual churches within the whole work of God, then we need to think about the redemption of humanity, renewal of creation and the coming of the kingdom. The question of how God relates to people and to his creation is central. As the systematic theologian Wilhelm Richebächer writes, God's mission can be seen in terms of encounter with Christ:

> The mission of the triune God is an invitation to life in all its fullness in the redeeming presence of the risen one. In the light of his resurrection, all previous encounters with God undergo a radical realignment through a power not available to human beings. These encounters can no longer be seen independently of the encounter with Christ. (2003, p. 596)

If one seeks evidence of the mission of God simply by looking for missionary practices of the church, then the crucial aspects of encounter with God will be missed. The whole work of God and character of God have to be taken into account. God's mission is centred on his encounter with his creation. This will affect how we think about church, moving us to start from the point of God reaching out to humanity and drawing back in – starting with encounter rather than practices. In another strand of his argument in *Reproducing Churches*, Lings too comes to this conclusion: 'I have become convinced that our thoughts about what the church should be like are best derived from Christ' (2017, p. 107). In the next chapter I will argue that the whole work of God can be approached by focusing on Christ, in particular in the way we approach atonement, and that this gives a framework for interpreting the actions of God in people's lives.

Kingdom

If mission is just one part of God's action in the world, perhaps a better theological starting point for the establishment of new ecclesial communities would be in a discussion of God's kingdom, as some writers have done, which can encompass ideas of mission. The Fresh Expressions organization themselves have made this connection: '[Fresh expressions] reflect the mission heart of God, they are a vehicle for proclaiming salvation and they are a means of making God's kingdom more real in today's world.'[4] Here the purpose of mission is seen to extend God's kingdom and the purpose of a new church – or indeed any church – is to advance the kingdom.

Jesus spoke a lot about the kingdom of God – or of heaven – as being near, having arrived and as still to be fully realized; it is found, and will come, both on earth and in heaven (cf. Mark 1.15; Luke 17.20–21; John 18.36). The coming of the kingdom sees the reign of Christ transform all of creation. Mission as a concept, therefore, sits within the idea of the kingdom. The mission is to advance the kingdom.

In 1984 the Anglican Consultative Council identified 'five marks of mission', which have since been adopted by the Anglican Church worldwide. They reflect a kingdom emphasis to mission. Naturally they include evangelism, conversion and discipleship, but extend to serving those in need, challenging and transforming unjust structures in society, and to stewarding and safeguarding creation.[5] These elements indicate that all things will one day be restored and brought within the reign of Christ, into God's kingdom. It can be argued that the mission of the Church is to participate in God's work of restoration. It is not unknown for fresh expressions to begin from one of these marks, with a kingdom approach to mission. For example, the Saturday Gathering, in Halifax, grew from a desire to respond to human need, out of a foodbank.[6] The organizers offered opportunities for prayer alongside the distribution of food packages, and found that people were becoming Christians as they were being prayed for by the team. However, these new Christians then found it difficult to integrate into small rural congregations that reflected a different culture from the people attending to foodbanks. This fresh expression almost started up by accident. Their starting point, the kingdom impulse to love and serve the needy, led into the formation of community and then church.

Despite such examples, John Hull critiqued the Fresh Expressions movement for promoting a mission that is church-shaped rather than a church that is mission-shaped (2006, pp. 1–4). His argument is based on an understanding of God's kingdom. Hull is in favour of fresh expressions but came out in force against the theological underpinnings of the initial *Mission-Shaped Church* report. He rightly claims that: 'The purpose or function of mission is to bring in the kingdom. In order to do this effectively, the mission has (among other things), a church' (p. 2). However, he then argues that *Mission-Shaped Church* concentrated too much on the creation of church communities at the expense of kingdom principles, resulting in this being the only outworking of fresh expression missional activity – mission has become church-shaped. For example, he writes: 'the poor are empowered not by having their own poor churches, but by escaping from poverty' (p. 33). He would have liked the report to have had deeper missiological foundations and a greater emphasis on kingdom. It must be noted that there has been much theology written about fresh expressions since 2006 when Hull published his booklet.

Hull's critique only has weight if one takes that view that fresh expressions practitioners have a specific approach to the kingdom – that the kingdom and Church are indistinguishable. I do not believe this is the predominant view of practitioners. Several mistakes can be made when it comes to thinking about the kingdom and the Church, which Moynagh has helpfully outlined (2012, pp. 101–2). The Church is not the kingdom, neither is the Church the extent of mission. One error, at one end of the spectrum, is to think of the role of the Church as 'pulling in souls' – however that may be done – from the world to the Church for salvation. This could be called a church-shaped kingdom: the Church is the kingdom when it is being true to its mission. The danger of this viewpoint is that it can cause the Church to ignore what God is doing in the world, and become so focused on conversion that it takes no notice of other things Jesus was passionate about, such as social injustices, poverty, stewardship of creation and so on. The other extreme is to think of the kingdom as synonymous with all of creation. This viewpoint sees Christ already present in the world but maintains that the task of the Church is simply to recognize, embrace and celebrate it. This has the effect of diminishing the role of the Church to simply pointing out signs of the kingdom rather than having a transformative effect on the world. The danger here is that people may never be brought to encounter the transformative love of God for themselves, and the Church may not feel it has a role to play in helping to change unjust or difficult aspects of society. These two extremes are dangers for both fresh expressions and traditional churches.

A better approach to thinking about the kingdom traces a middle path. Moynagh and others argue that the Church is there to critique the world, to find signs of the kingdom and to direct those signs to Christ (2012, pp. 102–4; Cray, 2012, pp. 14–15). This could be called a kingdom-shaped Church. Given that the kingdom is present but not fully realized, the kingdom is present wherever the Spirit is at work. In this sense the kingdom is already in the world as the Spirit is active in the world. However, the Church is also seen as the first fruits of the kingdom. It offers the kingdom to the world and receives the kingdom from the world where the Spirit is working. Together, this kingdom is advanced. The Church is therefore expected to grow, but this growth may come from unexpected places where the Spirit is working. One cannot expect God to move solely within the structures the Church has developed, and new life has often sprung out of surprising contexts or movements. The Church, therefore, needs to be contextual wherever the Spirit is working. This approach to the kingdom allays the fears of John Hull that fresh expressions result in a mission that is church-shaped, as instead fresh expressions seek to follow the Spirit in growing the kingdom of God. This kingdom-shaped approach gives the flexibility required to be contextual in each location.

One of the advantages of using God's kingdom as a theological starting point is that it forces those leading the new contextual church to focus on God's action. The church is there to advance the kingdom but also to be involved in kingdom-advancing work outside of the church, both offering to and receiving the kingdom from the world. Pioneers are often judged on creating church, on numbers coming to a gathering, on what happens when they meet or on numbers coming to faith. Of course these are all good things. However, this kingdom approach enables the value to be seen in activities that take place in the community that may not appear to lead to conversions or an increase in worshippers but are kingdom work nonetheless.

Although thinking about the Church in relation to the kingdom can offer some valuable insights into the Church's countercultural calling, its usefulness as an overarching foundation for new ecclesial communities can be questioned. Lings highlights the effectiveness of the idea in the world of the Roman Empire that Jesus inhabited, but notes that after the resurrection the apostles tended to focus on talking mostly about Jesus' death and resurrection rather than the kingdom (2017, p. 107).[7] Added to this he questions how kingdom language is received in cultures that have been democracies or republics for some time. I have found this to be true in my preaching. Although, once grasped, the concept is a powerful one for Christians, as it is linked with our primary identity and allegiance as being citizens of heaven, under the rule of Christ the King, I have found that the concept of kingdom usually needs to be explained in some detail before getting to this point. Although the UK has a monarchy, in our democracy the sovereign's power is limited, meaning that citizens usually do not see themselves as subjects in a kingdom. Even when such a concept is understood, defining what is or is not kingdom work can be tricky. Much better is to focus on Jesus and his place as the Saviour, Christ, and Lord. Lings writes: 'Without the King, the kingdom is vacuous . . . Without Christ's incarnation, atonement and the spiritual transformation brought by an encounter with him, kingdom language is in danger of becoming powerless idealism' (2017, p. 107).

Spirit

Before I develop the argument for a Christ-focused, cross-shaped foundation for new contextual churches, there is one more important line of thinking that must be discussed. Following the Spirit is a key driver in thinking about strategies for mission and church growth in our present age. In fact the former Archbishop of Canterbury, Rowan Williams, without whom the Fresh Expressions movement would not have gained so much traction, reportedly described mission as 'finding out where the Spirit is at work, and joining in' (cited in Kim, 2010, p. 51). God acts in the world through his Holy Spirit. The charismatic and pentecostal traditions also take the Spirit seriously, both in his impulse to engage in mission and in the encounter with God that comes through the Spirit. Some have argued that for charismatics and pentecostals the whole point of church is to encounter the Spirit and be equipped by him, a filling up and a sending out (Albrecht, 1996, pp. 107–25; Anderson, 2004, pp. 187–98). Can one describe the church according to the Holy Spirit, and would this be useful as a theological foundation for thinking about fresh expressions? It is the Spirit who calls the church to be holy and set apart, who works in the lives of believers transforming them to Christlikeness, and who leads the church out to witness to Christ, often to unexpected places. It was the Spirit who initially anointed the disciples, empowered them to speak and called them to see the church as a community of all cultures (Acts 2—11). The Spirit also has a unique role in the ministry of reconciliation, calling people to peace with God and into peaceful communion with one another. In one sense the Spirit might be seen as the instigator of mission and *koinonia*, while in another the work of the Spirit can be thought of within the work of the Trinity as a whole. Although the Spirit's role is unique and essential, the usefulness of this role as a starting point for conceptualizing new contextual churches is limited. Positively, thinking about the Spirit can lead to an emphasis on encounter with God and can drive the pioneer to seek the places where God is already active in the world. However, in all these things the Spirit's role is to point to Christ and his work, so a theology based on Christology may be better.

Which way forward?

Each of the doctrines outlined above is useful and should be thought about when it comes to new ecclesial communities, although none can be regarded as the final word. At Berrywood, although we did not consciously spend time unpacking these doctrines before we began, elements of each were present. Our approach sprang out of a desire for mission and community with the key value of hospitality, which led us into certain practices. However, when it came to assessing whether what we were doing was working, these doctrines were unable to help us get to an answer. Yes, we were doing mission, but what criteria would we use to ascertain whether this mission was advancing the kingdom? Yes, we were building community, but again this appeared to be a slippery concept. I have also outlined above the difficulties of aligning church practices with the inner workings of the Godhead. The final project milestone of the four that were outlined at the beginning of the project, to which I was held to account by my steering group throughout my time, focused on vision, sustainability of resources, leadership and finance among other things (see Withington, 2011). These are all-important things in new contextual churches, but are drawn from management thinking rather than theology.

After leaving Berrywood, contemplating what we had done, I wanted to find a foundation that would be able to articulate what was happening in theological language. As I have described, the theological starting points of Trinity, mission, kingdom and the Spirit are all insufficient in their own ways. I do not like the word 'success' when it comes to describing church, as it has all kinds of worldly connotations. However, I wanted to find a theological language that could be applied to fresh expressions to determine whether they, in some sense, are being successful. Numbers do matter but this cannot be the whole story. I believe the Church is to grow, and the role of the Church is, among other things, to bring those who do not yet know Christ to him. But numbers alone cannot be the only yardstick of success. We need to talk about God and his purposes, and therefore we need to come through Christ, the means by which God revealed himself to the world.

Notes

1 See www.moot.uk.net for a full account of their current events and activities. The Fresh Expressions organization wrote up an account of their approach in 2010, when Mobsby was still the leader: 'Moot': www.community.sharetheguide.org/stories/moot; accessed 17 Nov. 2017.

2 See Zizioulas (1985, pp. 149ff.) for the development of this argument.

3 For those who want to follow this line of argument, the Catholic theologian Hans Urs von Balthasar has written that even those who do not acknowledge God could be said to be participating in the relationship of God: 'The creature's "No", its wanting to be autonomous without acknowledging its origin, must be located within the Son's all embracing "Yes" to the Father, in the Spirit' (1994, p. 329). This is a form of participation that could lead to the 'no' becoming a 'yes'. While this argument is perhaps a little tenuous, it does leave space for the idea that creating community in secular environments could be regarded as *koinonia*.

4 'Why do Fresh Expressions Matter?': https://freshexpressions. org.uk/guide-me/going-deeper-3-why-do-fresh-expressions-matter; accessed 6 Oct. 2017.

5 'Marks of Mission', The Anglican Communion: www.anglican communion.org/identity/marks-of-mission.aspx; accessed 15 Nov. 2017.

6 'Saturday Gathering', Christians Together in Calderdale: http:// christianstogether.org.uk/saturdaygathering; accessed 28 Feb. 2017.

7 The word 'kingdom' is only mentioned eight times in the book of Acts. These are mostly in sermons where the preacher is talking to Jews or those who have already become Christians.

5

A cross-shaped church

About four years into my post, roughly two and a half years after we first started meeting for regular worship, I realized that despite our continued activity, we had unintentionally stopped making new connections with people in the community and that numbers in our worship gathering had plateaued. Although we had plenty of reach into different aspects of community life, we seemed to be at capacity. Sunday worship by this time occurred three times a month and attracted about 20 people, including children, each week (with roughly 35 people in total who came regularly). We had a core group of people in each of our other ministries, such as the midweek craft group for parents and pre-schoolers, the men's Curry and Questions discussion evenings and the Friday-morning Bible and Bubbles women's discussion group. Each of those was going well; we were investing in the relationships and helping some to grow in faith. But it seemed that the number of people we were reaching had levelled out. Despite this, using some of the theological concepts discussed in the last chapter, we could argue that we were succeeding. We were doing kingdom work, engaging in mission, and if we had wanted to apply the relationships of the Trinity to what we were doing, it would have been possible. However, none of these concepts adequately described what was actually going on.

In the last chapter I examined how some of the key theological concepts that have been used to describe fresh expressions may affect the shape and priorities of the church. In this chapter I suggest that we need to ask questions about God and how he relates to the world, in order to work out what emphasis any individual fresh expression should have and to describe what is happening in a church where God is at work. I will argue that this is best done through an understanding of the atonement. This cross-shaped approach will then be developed further in Chapter 6.

A Jesus-centred Church

At the beginning of the Gospels, Jesus is described as the fulfilment of God's dealings with his people in the Old Testament. Matthew places Jesus squarely in the line of descendants that flows from Abraham and the fathers of Israel through the line of King David (Matt. 1.1–17). Then, in his telling of the story from the birth of Jesus to the ministry of John the Baptist, he uses the Old Testament to demonstrate that Jesus is indeed the anticipated Messiah and the ruler of Israel (Matt. 1.18 — 2.12). Luke emphasizes the unique circumstances of Jesus' birth alongside all the angelic and prophetic proclamations that are made about the Christ. The song of Mary (Luke 1.46–55) and the praises of Simeon in the Temple (3.29–32) both connect Jesus with the saving work of the God of Israel. Mark begins his Gospel by stating that the account he is about to give is the beginning of the 'good news', or 'gospel' of Jesus (Mark 1.1). The good news encompasses all that is to follow – his birth, life, teaching, signs and miracles, death and resurrection. This is by no means an exhaustive list but it illustrates that Christ is at the centre of how God engages with the world. Since his ascension, Christ has left us his Holy Spirit, but it is to Christ that the Spirit witnesses.

Because God engages with the world through Christ, should not this knowledge be the basis of our understanding of how God interacts in the world today and how he uses the Church to that end? In academic language this would be called a Christological ecclesiology – a Christ-centred understanding of church.

The Church's role in the world is shaped by Christ's actions. Paul makes this link when he argues in his first letter to the church in Corinth that: 'God was reconciling the world to himself in Christ . . . And he has committed to us the message of reconciliation' (2 Cor. 5.19). Christ's task of reconciliation has been passed on to the church. Therefore the role of the church is to witness to and participate in Christ's work, as Christ is the means of God's engagement with the world.

The former Archbishop of Canterbury, Rowan Williams, made this link too, speaking of fresh expressions:

> Church is the event of Jesus' presence with its characteristic effect of gathering people around him and making them see one another differently as they see him . . . The church is what happens when Jesus is there, there received and recognised. (Williams, 2004)

This loose definition of church links the characteristics of church with the presence and action of Jesus. Christ gives content to the mission, doctrine, practices, experience and message of the Church. What would church look like if we focused our practices on the concerns of Christ?

Karl Barth's Christ-centred Church

One of the most notable theologians of the twentieth century was Karl Barth. His major work is the four-volume masterpiece of doctrine, *Church Dogmatics*, written between 1932 and 1968. It is usually published in 14 separate books. The four volumes cover the subjects of the Word of God, God himself, creation and reconciliation. In the fourth volume on reconciliation, Barth gives an extensive discussion of what it is to be church. Reconciliation is, of course, one of the outcomes of Christ's work. Barth places his discussion of the Church here because he believes the Church is fundamentally about Christ. It is not simply a collection of individuals gathered around a common interest, but is divinely established and displays something of God's purposes for humanity. It is therefore set apart to serve the world and witness to God (*Church Dogmatics* (hereafter *CD*), II.2, 197).

If church is centred on reconciliation, we need to ask what this is and how God reconciles. Barth describes reconciliation as the restoration and resumption of the relationship between God and humanity to its original purpose, through Christ (*CD* IV.1, 22; IV.3.1, 38–9). In other words, God is bringing all things back to himself through Christ, restoring the relationship between himself and creation to be as he originally intended it to be. As this happens through Christ, the Christian life therefore has a Christ-shape to it. And as each believer is reconciled to God through Christ, communities of Christian believers become 'concrete and grounded' forms of Christ's existence in the world (*CD* IV.1, 661; IV.2, 655). Put simply, Christ exists in the world through communities of believers who make up the Church. Paul calls this the body of Christ (1 Cor. 12.12–31). As such, Barth argues, the Church exists to witness to Christ's work (*CD* IV.1, 150). But Barth is clear that this role is solely as a witness to Christ:

> They have not to assist or add to the being and work of their living Saviour who is the Lord of the world, let alone to replace it by their own work. The community is not a prolongation of His incarnation, His death and resurrection, the acts of God and their revelation. It has not to do these things. It has to witness to them. It is its consolation that it can do this. Its marching-orders are to do it. (*CD* IV.1, 317–318)

Because Christ's work is complete, Barth sees that the only task for the Church is in witnessing to Christ, not participating in Christ's work. He claims the Church cannot assist Christ in the reconciliation of the world because this is Christ's work alone. The Church can make a difference and bring about change in the world, but these are merely signs of God's work through the Church, not signs of the Church's work. They witness to Christ's work rather than contribute to it (*CD* IV.3.2, 729, 835–6, 841–2).

While elements of this sound a little complex, particularly where the line between Christ's work and the Church's is concerned, what Barth has done is actually quite simple: he has focused the Church on Jesus Christ. Often we can talk ourselves into theological side-issues as we consider how the Church is to approach important issues that can be seen in the world. We can argue that the Church should be about mission, fellowship, community-building or following the Spirit. All those are true. But at its heart we must return to the foundation and declare that the Church is first and foremost about Jesus Christ – his person, works and power. Everything else flows from this. Where I differ from Barth, if I may be so bold, is to caution against his reduction of the task of the Church to mere witness or proclamation to God's action, rather than participation in it. Certainly I believe the Church is a witness to Christ, but it is also more than that. Through the Spirit, the Church participates in the works of Christ and is empowered to bring about transformation, through Christ. Transformation comes about because of God's work (rather than as a result of our work), but the Church as the body of Christ joins with him in this work in the world, bringing people to the fulfilment he effected in Christ's incarnation, death and resurrection.

So Barth's discussion of the Church, its work and its shape is rooted firmly in the gospel. This makes a lot of sense – surely the Church should be about proclaiming and living out the fullness of the good news of Christ, and surely the gospel should shape how we do church? Barth's starting point of reconciliation is useful too, but we need to remember that reconciliation is just one of the major actions God puts into effect through Jesus' life, death and resurrection. God does more than this. In Christ, God also saves, justifies, sanctifies, redeems, restores, transforms and forgives. They all form part of the doctrine of atonement. When people begin a relationship with God they experience one or more of these actions, although they may not put it in these words. What if we were to expand Barth's vision from reconciliation to include all of these actions and ask what the doctrine of atonement, in its broadest sense, could offer to our discussion of what church should be like?

Atonement and church

Atonement is one of those things Christians like to argue about. Many different theories of atonement have fallen in and out of favour throughout history. I am not going to promote one over the other here. Not only is this beyond the scope of this book but I believe that most if not all the atonement theories have some merits, and can be supported by Scripture. It is, however, important to have a broad definition of atonement to work with. Atonement refers to the saving of all creation by the Holy Trinity through the life, death and resurrection of Jesus Christ. The goal of atonement is that all of creation may be united in praise for God the Father. Atonement involves God taking the initiative to draw all things back to himself.[1]

For a theory of atonement to be valid, a couple of elements need to be present. First, the initiative must begin with God; God must do something for humanity that we cannot do for ourselves, otherwise Jesus' death would not be necessary. Second, it must adequately deal with sin, otherwise there is nothing to atone for. Therefore the example theory of atonement, which claims that Jesus inspires positive moral improvement through his life, death and teaching, is not a valid theory, as it does not deal with sin and therefore ultimately Christ's death becomes unnecessary (McKnight, 2007, p. 114). Even with these two constraints, there is still plenty of scope for variation. As mentioned above, Christ's atonement achieves for humanity reconciliation, forgiveness, sanctification, redemption, restoration, transformation and salvation; different theories emphasize these elements to different degrees.

This almost gets us to a point where we can start examining the theories to determine what they can contribute to church practice, but not quite, as there is disagreement among writers over how many distinct theories there are and even whether theories themselves are the most helpful way to think about atonement. For example, in their book *Recovering the Scandal of the Cross*, Joel Green and Mark Baker suggest five images of the atonement that contribute to our understanding of the theories. These are justification, redemption, reconciliation, sacrifice and victory, and are borrowed from the fields of law, commerce, personal relationships, worship and war (2000, p. 23). Other writers either prioritize one theory over the others or are content to give them equal priority and live with the tensions between them. In *A Community Called Atonement*, Scot McKnight investigates the main theories, the biblical themes, and images of the atonement before attempting to unify them all in his own overarching theory. His final offering ends up being cumbersome but he does make some helpful points about how his theories, themes and images relate to church practice (2007, pp. 107–14). Having said this, most writers agree that there are core biblical images – justification, redemption, reconciliation, sacrifice and victory – with one or two additions or variations.

Another complication is that theories are also often divided into two camps: the subjective and the objective. Although this appears to make the subject more complex, thinking about atonement in this way can help us locate where the Church fits into God's work. The objective concentrates on God's act whereas the subjective emphasizes active human participation in God's action. Objective theories stress that Jesus' death achieves something and is of value in itself, be it sacrifice for sin or deflection of God's wrath. The human element is almost incidental in these theories. Subjective theories emphasize the human side of God's work, such as the transformation of the person. In practice, I think it is not helpful to divide theories in this way, as most have both subjective and objective sides to them. However, thinking of how the subjective and objective aspects of Christ's work relate can indicate where the place of the Church should be. Barth describes these two elements as the history of Jesus Christ (objective) and the history of those throughout time who participate in Christ (subjective). For Barth, the Church exists where the two histories coincide – where Christ's work meets human response. If we consider two perpendicular axes, with human sin on the horizontal and the work of Christ on the vertical, at the intersection of the two the divine act of God through Christ meets with human history. This is where Christ's work overlaps with human history and where he is at work in and through people (*CD* IV.1, 643).

Because Barth's axes clearly connect the actions of God in the atonement with the Church, I suggest that so long as a theory of the atonement is theologically valid, it has something to say to the Church. I do not believe that we need to prioritize one over the others as all are present in Scripture. In each theory the place where Christ's work meets human response will have something valuable to say to the Church. Next I will examine the work of three atonement writers to explore how the writing and preferred theory of each affects the shape of church. These particular writers have been chosen because they have made connections between atonement theories and the practice of the Church – not something many writers on this subject have attempted.

Christus Victor

The first writer I will consider is Greg Boyd, a pastor and theologian who is sympathetic to the emerging church movement in the USA (which shares missional traits with the fresh expressions movement). He favours the *Christus Victor* theory of atonement, seeing it as having priority over other theories.

Christus Victor originated from the teachings of the church fathers, before falling out of favour for centuries. It was reintroduced – and named – by the Swedish Lutheran theologian Gustav Aulén in the early twentieth century (Aulén, 1931).[2] *Christus Victor* understands the atonement as a divine conflict culminating in a cosmic victory of Christ over Satan and the evil powers of the world that keep humanity in bondage. Jesus the divine human is seen as the second Adam, who binds Satan in a show of non-violent force, by submitting to and overcoming death. Using imagery from Mark telling of the parable of the strong man (Mark 3.23–27), Jesus metaphorically enters the house (death) of the strong man (Satan) to overcome him. Jesus' death also recapitulates, 'sums up' or replays the whole of humanity in their death (in Adam), and their capture by Satan. This moves humanity from being identified with Adam, with sin bringing death and separation from

God, to being identified 'in Christ', being made righteous and able to participate in life with Christ (see Romans 5). Human death has been replayed and renewed with a new ending: communion with God by the Holy Spirit. In communion with God we are joined with others who also have communion with God. Thus Christ's victory is linked directly with life in the community of the Church. Paul's encouragement to the community of Ephesian believers (plural) to take up the 'armour of God' of faith, peace, righteousness and salvation lends itself to this theory (Eph. 6.10–18).

Without rejecting the other atonement theories outright, Boyd gives *Christus Victor* priority, as he claims the cosmic significance of Christ's work encompasses everything else (2006, pp. 24ff.). Individual salvation is placed in the context of Christ's ultimate cosmic victory. Humanity is reconciled to God because all things in the cosmos are reconciled. Humanity is considered holy to God because all the powers against God are defeated. The believer participates in his victory, which enables a victory over personal and social issues. According to Boyd, salvation is much larger than simply overcoming personal sin and avoiding hell. In *Christus Victor*, salvation is from God's enemies, from destruction, from brokenness and the human inability to live holy lives. Salvation is from idolatrousness and meaninglessness. Crucially, humanity is not only saved *from* those things but is saved *to* participate with Christ – and with others who participate in Christ – in love, joy, power, peace and the reign of God.

How can *Christus Victor* be useful to the contemporary Church? First, it can be useful in how we talk about God, moving the conversation about the gospel on from simply being a remedy for personal sin to consider the larger context of evil. The gospel can then be articulated in a manner that seems more relevant to contemporary ears. Jürgen Moltmann, whose thinking was greatly influenced by his experiences of the Second World War, was one such writer. Moltmann saw the forces of evil and death that were clearly on display in the world, and concluded that individualized accounts of the atonement would not do as they do not account for the sheer greatness of sin and the fallen state of the whole world (1990, pp. 171–81). *Christus Victor* avoids this charge, as it takes evil, and Christ's victory over it, seriously.

There is also an argument that more recent contemporary society does not have much of a concept of personal sin. As a word, 'sin' has come to refer to things that are a little bit naughty but still allowable, such as food that is slightly indulgent or actions that may have been perceived to be off-limits in the past but are now widely practised, such as premarital sex. Genuine sins are perceived to be limited to other people and include crimes such as murder, paedophilia or terrorism. Before I studied theology I worked in the computer industry. I remember having a conversation in a pub with a group of work colleagues after a game of football, when the topic of discussion turned to religion, and sin in particular. One colleague remarked that he genuinely could not think of a single example of a time when he had 'sinned'. It perhaps was not the most fruitful conversation but it does illustrate my point – since sin is misunderstood, communicating the gospel exclusively from a starting point of personal sin can be flawed.[3] However, although sin may not be recognized, most people recognize the presence of evil in the world, clearly evident in daily news broadcasts and typified by increasingly common terrorist attacks. Perhaps evil is a better place to start in engaging apologetically. People also have an awareness of personal shame, which may or may not manifest itself as guilt. An atonement theory that takes seriously the powers of evil yet still highlights Jesus as the fully human Saviour facing all the temptations and sufferings of humanity, but overcoming them, is surely attractive and can alleviate shame. Perhaps starting with the benefits of being 'in Christ' and the joy that comes from participation in fullness of life, rather than focusing on Christ's substitution for sin and the promise of forgiveness that comes with the territory of other atonement theories, will be a more fruitful point of connection with young people today.

The second way *Christus Victor* can be useful to the church today is that it meets another contemporary need, for authentic and faithful community. On our new-build development it was striking how few people knew those who lived around them. With no pre-existing community and little in the way of community groups enabling people to meet others who lived nearby, most had initially built their friendship networks through existing relationships or work colleagues. However, we found that when a first child arrived, residents began to notice their lack of connection with those who lived immediately around them and began to want to make friends. *Christus Victor* emphasizes participation in the community of Christ, which invites opportunities for deep and authentic communities. As Brian Gregory, another *Christus Victor* proponent writes:

> What we need is not a better way to *communicate* the atonement of the narrative of God's work in history; we need a church that is faithful to its calling to *embody* the narrative in its very way of life. (Gregory, 2015, p. 157; emphasis original)

Since the church is to embody Christ's victory in its community, we could argue that if we cannot see it being embodied then the church has failed. *Christus Victor* enables themes of justification and sanctification, which are often spoken about in individualistic terms, to be set within the greater perspective of the return of Christ and participation in the new community of the saved. If we look through the pages of the Gospels it is easy to see that this community is inclusive of all kinds of people who were and often are marginalized: the poor, outcasts, women, sinners, the suffering. Jesus reincorporated outcasts into community, such as Zacchaeus the tax collector, who was invited into table-fellowship (Luke 19.1–10). The ten lepers who were healed were readmitted into society. That one of them was a Samaritan is further evidence of Jesus' reaching out to outsiders (Luke 17.11–19). The demon-possessed man who was living among the graves in the region of the Gerasenes is liberated from his affliction and brought back into community (Mark 5.1–20). Jesus' life, death and resurrection inaugurated a new reality and a new community characterized by freedom, inclusivity, equality, peace and joy, which became the Church. Therefore we can say the church is a pointer towards what God's kingdom will be like after Jesus returns, and is there to witness to the salvation of Christ in the present age – through words and actions – until this new age is fully realized. Signs of this kingdom are in the present age; the church can live out and point to these signs. In Western society, where local community relations are diminishing, this aspect of *Christus Victor* can offer much-needed close-knit community and support.

A third concept that *Christus Victor* can offer to the church is liberation. Jesus spoke of oppressive forces of sin, death and Satan in a cosmic language. For example, following the return of the 72 from their mission trip, Jesus remarks that he 'saw Satan fall like lightning from heaven' (Luke 10.18). This spiritual image of liberation was illustrated in more concrete instances of liberation in the people Jesus came across. The widowed woman is liberated from her grief and poverty in the raising of her son off the funeral bier (Luke 7.11–16), as are Mary and Martha, unmarried sisters who would have been facing an uncertain future after the death of their brother Lazarus (John 11).

That Jesus Christ liberates humanity from bondage to evil and sin has many parallels in contemporary culture. Gustavo Gutiérrez is a South American theologian who argues that the gospel is liberating in concrete and practical ways. To him, *Christus Victor* implies the transformation of humanity (1988, pp. 133–4; 147–61). Freedom from bondage to sin implies that people's life situations will change. The consequences for the church are practical. First, the church is required to speak up for justice against oppressive structures, and against the powers, stories and structures that maintain the status quo. Of course, these will differ in each context. But simply standing up against these things is not enough. This is why, second, the church must proclaim the alternative vision of the good news of Christ, his message of liberation, and live out the transformation, not just speak about it. Wherever this happens, the community of believers are able to create just social relationships that demonstrate the unity and diversity of Christ. Thus

Christus Victor suggests that the church needs to be involved in all forms of liberation, from global injustices to personal addictions, making a difference in practical and spiritual ways. In whatever culture or subculture a new ecclesial community finds itself emerging, there are sure to be issues of liberation to stand up against and transform.

Christus Victor has much to offer the church in how it thinks about practices, but this is just one theory among many. How might other theories or images of atonement be applied to the practices of the church?

Atonement and mission

The second atonement writer I will engage with is John Driver, whose book *Understanding the Atonement for the Mission of the Church* makes a clear link between doctrine and practice (Driver, 1986). Driver was an American missionary to South America and the Caribbean who served as a professor in several Latin American seminaries. Preferring to think in terms of images rather than theories, he lists ten images of the atonement and makes missional applications from each.

For example, he expands the idea of sacrifice, something Paul developed from Old Testament Passover and sin-offering imagery, which Jews would have understood in terms of redemption and forgiveness (2 Cor. 5.21). The writer of Hebrews takes this imagery and applies it as a once-and-for-all eternal sacrifice by Jesus, bringing eternal redemption to the believer. Because the world of Christ impacts the believer, the atonement image of sacrifice then becomes an image for understanding Christian community. Believers demonstrate self-sacrifice in the way they live out their lives together, praise God, serve others and share (1986, pp. 144–6).[4] So although, as Christians, we can understand Jesus' sacrifice on a spiritual level, there is a practical outworking of it too. We must be careful to avoid the tendency to separate the spiritual aspects of faith and belief from our practical living.

Sacrifice of some form is of course present in all societies, usually not in a good way. Many groups are used to sacrificing

or scapegoating an individual or group of people for the perceived benefit of the many. It can be argued that the President
of the USA, Donald Trump, swept to power off the back of the
scapegoating of immigrants. Some of his first actions were to
introduce executive orders banning certain nationalities from
travelling to the USA, in the understanding that it would benefit the security of the country. Similarly, in the aftermath of the
Iraq war in 2003, many argue that Dr David Kelly, an expert
on biological warfare and a former United Nations weapons
inspector, was singled out by the British government to take
the fall for political failures. Two days after being aggressively
questioned by a parliamentary committee about the content
of a government dossier, he was found to have committed sui-
cide. In this case, his scapegoating was too much for him. It is
not uncommon to see this cycle of scapegoating played out in
order to protect the interests of the powerful.

Seeing this pattern in everyday life, the French philosopher
René Girard proposed that a repeating cycle of scapegoating
can be seen in human history, which results in a redemptive but
never-resolving cycle of sacrifice – the scapegoating achieves its
end in calming the situation for a short time but is then required
again with another unfortunate victim. Jesus' death puts a stop
to this once and for all (Girard, 2001, pp. 154–60). Since Jesus
was delivered as 'an atoning sacrifice for our sins' (1 John 4.10),
as the ultimate sacrifice to end all sacrifices, humanity no longer
needs to sacrifice or scapegoat victims in any way.

The practical application of this is for church communities
to be diverse and free from fear. People can be different, things
can go wrong, yet the unity and make-up of the community is
not affected. Nobody needs to be sacrificed or scapegoated for
any reason because Christ has been the one complete sacrifice
and he has united all believers in him. Believers can then join
church communities formed around obedient trust and mutual
cooperation, without any fear that they will be rejected for
whatever reason. At Berrywood we found that a strength in one
of our morning groups lay in the culture that was created, so
that participants were able to share deep and troubling issues,
even failures. Because there was mutual trust and cooperation,

members did not fear being rejected by the community. This allowed deep healing to take place. I will argue later that the healing that occurred was an experience of atonement.

Another atonement image of reconciliation that Driver considers is reconciliation, which can also offer a practical application to the church. A key passage in the New Testament speaks of Jesus' death reconciling humanity once and for all to God and entrusting his followers with the 'ministry of reconciliation' (cf. 2 Cor. 5.11–20). Driver asserts that this ministry is achieved and concluded, but is ongoing and still in the process of being realized, and will only be fully completed when Jesus returns (1986, pp. 181–2). Jesus brings all people back into relationship with God and, in entrusting us with that ministry, the church plays a part in it. Therefore the church is to embody reconciliation. As it is God's covenant community, we must live as those reconciled to each other, living out the Christian characteristics of holiness and blamelessness that are emphasized in the New Testament letters (cf. Col. 1.21–22; Eph. 1.4; 5.25–27). This ministry of reconciliation is not just to be demonstrated within the church but actively pursued by it, as an act of mission. Our ministry of reconciliation involves both drawing others into a reconciled relationship with God and facilitating reconciliation between people.

I could follow these lines of reasoning for other atonement images too, such as adoption, justification, redemption, victory and liberation, as Driver does. Applying them to Christian community similarly impacts the shape and priorities of church in every area of life. Of course, the exact shape will vary depending on context, but I would expect a church that pursues these priorities to stand out clearly from the surrounding culture, even if that new contextual church has emerged from within the culture. Churches will be communities who love and forgive as God has done. They will offer a place for fellowship and to experience communion with the Father and Son. They will also work towards bringing freedom and justice for all, living out kingdom ethics. They will minister to the whole person, not just the spiritual, reflecting the cosmic aspect of Christ's victory. Finally, they will be visible as a confessing community, ambassadors to the kingdom of God in the world. As they are shaped around these things, they will commit energy and resources in pursuit of these things in ways that may appear countercultural.

Atonement and forms of the church

The third atonement writer I will engage with is the American systematic theologian Peter Schmiechen, who concretely links theories of atonement with shape of the church. Like John Driver and others, he acknowledges that no single theory is able to accomplish everything that is attested to in Scripture regarding the atonement (2005, pp. 5–8). Like Barth, he agrees that all thinking about church needs to start with Christ:

> It is difficult to have confidence if one does not know what to promote regarding Christ. Thus at the heart of the churches' struggle to find their identity and mission are the Christological questions posed by the life, death and resurrection of Jesus. (2005, p. 245)

The main thrust of Schmiechen's argument is that the theology and mode of atonement communicated – and demonstrated – affects the form of the church (2005, pp. 353–7). For example, he claims that concentration on Christ's incarnation leads to a sacramental understanding of church. A theology that emphasizes the truth of Scripture and an individual's response to faith – most often communicated with a justification or penal-substitution theory of atonement – results in a Church that is teaching-based. Different atonement theories can affect the outworking of church with regard to how sacraments and practices are understood, how Christians are encouraged to respond to Christ, what the role of the Holy Spirit should be, how one participates in community, how the church engages in service to others or how it shows solidarity with the suffering. Although one might quibble with some of Schmiechen's details, he is surely right in saying that a change in the theology that is communicated and lived out can change the shape of the church.

In *Defining the Church for Our Time* he develops his ideas, focusing his Christ-centred theology on Christ's return rather than the cross (Schmiechen, 2012). This is still a Christ-centred theology but focusing on a different aspect of Christ's work. Taking inspiration from the seventh-century Northumbrian monk Bede, according to whom 'Christ is the morning star who when the night of this world is past brings to his saints the promise of the light of life and opens everlasting day' (Bede, Commentary on Revelation, 2.18), Schmiechen writes that the promise of Christ's return offers hope for the present. The morning star indicates that the night is ending and a new dawn is on the horizon. The Church is therefore to be a community of hope. Christ's reign is to bring to fulfilment the work of God that has begun in Christ. He goes on to say:

> Christians are called to see, celebrate, and pray for the coming of the Kingdom – the very Kingdom Jesus announced and embodied. The new age, therefore, is not a time of preparation for Armageddon, but a time of missionary endeavor to preach, teach, and baptize (Matt. 28). In this time, the faithful are called to prepare and wait for the time when God will gather together all things in Christ (Eph. 1.10; cf. Col. 1.20) . . . [The Morning Star] not only draws us outside of ourselves, but draws us into Christ's future as recipients of grace and agents of reconciliation. (2012, pp. 112–3, 115)

If Christ's return is the gathering together of all things and the fulfilment of his work, it is not hard to see the broader aspects of atonement at work here. Christ will fulfil the work he began in the incarnation and completed on the cross. If Christ will ultimately reconcile all things, then his work of hope in the present – which has begun – is reconciliation. If believers will ultimately be justified, then the work of the present is in justification. The role the Church can play in this is through its activities and structures and in the lives of believers.

All this helps us in thinking about church growth and new forms of church, as a cross-centred emphasis can place the Church on a firm foundation. As I have noted, new churches can begin from wildly different starting points, including worship, preaching, small groups, service to others or evangelism. Sometimes they are started without assessing the underlying theology. Fresh Expressions thinking promotes listening to the context. Schmiechen's work stresses the importance of recognizing the theological starting points and the effect this has on church. Putting the theology and context alongside each other, the pioneer can ask questions such as: 'What does my strategy communicate about the gospel?' or 'Which understanding of the gospel do I want to communicate in this context, and therefore what practices should be used?' While this may not always be easy, as both the pioneer and the context will bring some cultural pre-understandings of the gospel (see van den Toren, 2010), an openness to explore one's own presumptions in the light of Scripture and the culture may lead to a more fruitful starting position that is true to the theological convictions of the pioneer and right for the needs of the context. It may lead both into a deeper experience of Christ. Of course, this is only possible if that openness exists, if the pioneer is willing to accept the value of many different atonement theories in the first place and to concede that different approaches suit different contexts.

Schmiechen has presented his argument in one direction – that our understanding of atonement dictates or affects the shape of the church. He is correct on this point. However, a truly cross-shaped church would want to begin with what God is doing, through Christ, in the lives of individuals and the community. He does allude to this in *Defining the Church* (2012, p. 120). From there one could ask what the practices of church should be relative to what God has done through Christ, is doing, and might do in our community. If we take the view that all atonement theories have merit, therefore God is in action through Christ in a wide variety of ways, we need to ask whether current practices of the church are giving space for our participation in these actions of God.

In this chapter we have seen how different approaches to atonement affect our understanding and practice in the church, and that there is much to be learned by considering each one. They each have an effect on what the church community does when it meets (preaching, sacrament, welcome, hospitality), and how these things may be done, as well as how the church relates and engages in the wider community (mission, justice, care for the poor). And, of course, when a congregation is dispersed in the workplace or social settings, the body of Christ is dispersed in the world in action. In the cross-shaped church, atoning actions affect individual believers in their daily lives outside the church as well as when the church gathers. The work of God through Christ, although achieved at a specific point in time on the cross, is ongoing as he acts daily in people's lives. These atoning actions in the present are worth exploring. In fresh expressions circles there is a saying that mission is 'finding out what God is doing and joining in'. In the next chapter I will start by asking what God is doing, where God can be found to be at work. I will then relate that to atonement thinking and ask how a church can recognize, participate and respond to that in its practices.

Notes

1 This definition is in line with other writers. For example, see Jenny Sankey (1995, pp. 93–110). For a clear unbiased overview of the different theories of atonement, Ben Pugh's book *Atonement Theories: A Way Through the Maze*, is hard to beat (Pugh, 2014). To read why some writers give one theory priority over the others, the edited collection *The Nature of the Atonement: Four Views* allows four writers each to promote their preferred theory and respond to the other three with points of agreement and critique (Beilby and Eddy, 2006).

2 There is some debate as to whether *Christus Victor* was the first recognized theory of atonement. Michael Gorman (2010, pp. 26–59) claims that a theory of covenant precedes *Christus Victor* in the New Testament and that this takes primacy over and encompasses the others.

3 For a longer discussion of this point, see Alan Mann (2005, pp. 31–43).

4 See also the following Bible passages, which link sacrifice with everyday life in some way: Rom. 12.1–2; 15.15–16; 1 Pet. 2.4–10; Heb. 10.19–25; 12.18–13.16.

6

Out of nothing

God can be seen to be at work through personal encounter. In the last chapter I discussed a number of approaches in which atonement can be seen to affect the shape of the ministry of the church. However, atonement is more immediate and concrete than simply being a theory to be applied. Whenever people share their testimony, they usually tell a personal story of what God has been doing in their life. Personal encounter is a more natural place to start when talking to others about God than pure doctrine, because these places of encounter are intimate and identity-forming. They alter the direction of people's lives and shape a believer's walk with God.

Sometimes they are stories of where God has helped them through a difficult time. At other times they are simply stories of God's blessing. But there is something about encountering people of faith that makes others aware of the possibility of encounter with God and helps them remember where God might have been in their lives. A few stories stand out. I described in Chapter 1 how I regularly used to visit the small-business owners on our housing development. One of the local shop owners was a friendly man who, when he wasn't seeing a client, was usually very happy to chat. Early on he told me about his seminal experience living on a kibbutz in Israel. He spoke very fondly of this time of close community and how it gave him an appreciation for 'higher things'. He was able to speak with some ease about this aspect of his life because it concerned a personal experience, whereas he might have struggled had he been trying to articulate a world view. I have no trouble calling this an experience of God.

While personal experience is usually the starting point, doctrine can help us make sense of these experiences; we believe in a God who acts through Christ, by the Spirit, in people's lives. As I argued in the previous chapter, this movement of God reaching out to humanity and drawing back in can be understood within the doctrine of atonement, in a broad sense. What would our understanding of church look like if we started our thinking from the place of encounter of God with humanity, from the experiences of God that occur in people's lives? This finds its centre in the incarnate, crucified, resurrected and ascended Christ.

The systematic theologian Eberhard Jüngel has written much on the doctrine of justification from a reformed viewpoint. Although he is writing a work of doctrine, his writing lends itself to a practical application focusing on the place of encounter. He speaks of justification rather than atonement; he sees this as the overarching category within which other aspects of atonement sit. Because this is where he starts, this is also where I will begin in exploring the place of encounter that humanity has with God, before expanding the applications out to other images of the atonement.

Jüngel's justification

Central to Jüngel's concept of justification are, as you might expect, sin and righteousness. In many ways he goes along on these counts with Luther, the father of reformed theology. Like the reformers, justification is in Christ alone, by grace alone, by Word alone, by faith alone. Concerning the word 'alone', Jüngel adds that humanity has nothing to offer when it comes to their own justification; it is entirely by the power and grace of God (2001, p. 148). It is only accessed by faith (and even this is a gift from God).

In English the word 'justification' has legal connotations. It is often described as the bestowing of God's justice, on Jesus, in our place, and the concurrent imparting of God's righteousness, through Jesus, on humanity. If I were to think of an illustration to highlight the concept, I might think of a courtroom in which God the Father sits in the judge's chair, with Jesus both as advocate/barrister and in the dock in our place. This is not always helpful, as it can portray God the Father as a dispassionate observer; the Father pronounces the judgement that would be on us were it not for the merciful Son. Linguistically, in both biblical Greek (the language in which the New Testament was written) and in German (the language in which Jüngel wrote), 'justice' and 'righteousness' have their root in the same word: *dikaios* in Greek; *gerecht* in German. The fact that there are two different words in English is an anomaly, as we take 'justice' from the Latin *iustitia* whereas 'righteousness' emerges from middle-English and Germanic roots. If 'justification' has legal overtones, 'righteousness', in English, is thought of as a state of being for a holy or pious person; it is more of a character trait. However, since they both come from the same word, this distinction may be unhelpful.

Jüngel still sees a legal aspect to justification – this has not disappeared completely – but he brings together God's justice with the more relational concept of God's righteousness. In doing this he distances the image a little from a courtroom setting (2001, pp. 47–9). Justification is not simply about a judge pronouncing a verdict over sins for laws broken (which emphasizes the wrongdoing and punishment). The dispute in the court is about God and his honour and about the worth of human beings. This causes us to ask questions of who this God is, why he judges, for what aims, and who humans are in relation to him. All of these questions centre on relationship; justification, or being made righteous, is ultimately about relationship, not law. Being 'just' is a description of how relationships are ordered – between humanity and God, humanity and one another, humanity and the natural environment, humanity and oneself. This echoes the relationships that were broken at the fall. The sins of Adam and Eve were ultimately about broken relationships rather than broken laws. The first feeling they experienced was shame, not guilt, as they realized they were naked and wanted to cover themselves up. Their first inclination was to try to hide themselves from God, revealing the broken relationship that had taken place (Gen. 3.7–10).

All of life's relationships consist of the four directions of towards God, others, ourselves and the natural environment. When they are in place and harmonious, justice and peace rule. Therefore justification is about the reordering of relationships.

As God has created for relationship (or, as Jüngel describes it, 'existence together' (2001, pp. 103ff.)), he has created humanity for relationship and plays the driving role in enabling these relationships to take place. He instituted a covenant so that people could be (re)joined in togetherness with him. This covenant was first with Adam, then with Abraham, Israel and finally, through Jesus, with all creation. God is there, present and active in relationship and responsible for that relationship.

In stark contrast to God's activity in creating and enabling relationship, Jüngel sees evil and sin as what challenges and divides that togetherness with God. Again he is removing sin from the traditional courtroom image of wrongdoing. He writes that sin is our 'compulsive urge towards such a lack of relationships, when self-actualization becomes an absolute' (2001, p. 55). Sin is when we attempt to define ourselves apart from the relationships – or togetherness – God has marked out for us. Paradoxically, this can come from within ourselves. He observes that we are our own worst enemies when our compulsive urge to self-reliance strikes at the very heart of what makes us whole, our relationship with God. In attempting to make ourselves whole through independence, we can cut ourselves off from the life-giving relationship that gives us wholeness. Sin can manifest itself in self-deception and culminate in a self-reliance that leads to a lack of trust and therefore a break in relationship between the individual and God, themselves and others: 'The void, the emptiness of sin is made tangible in the form of a *disruption and destruction of the relationships* in which all togetherness takes place and without which existing things cannot exist' (Jüngel, 2001, pp. 112–13; emphasis original). This is where the idea of nothingness comes in. Of course, God created all things *ex nihilo*, out of nothing. Before creation there was only a void of chaos and darkness. Jüngel contests that this void of nothingness is able to find being within creation, in the form of sin. It breaks into God's good creation, which threatens the whole good order of things (2001, p. 112). In fact he claims that this nothingness within creation is actually worse than the nothingness that existed before creation, as it represents a loss of the good relationships and identity God has brought into being. He describes it as a negative nothingness because it gives the appearance of being something, even though it is not (1989, pp. 107–8). Sin is deceptive. It purports to being something fulfilling that can be relied on, whereas it actually leads to emptiness.

From within this nothingness, any attempts at self-realization can ultimately only be futile. We become unable to achieve the reordering of relationships by our own effort. We are not able to create an identity that can be relied on. We even become unable to call out to God. Jüngel calls this a state of speechlessness which, unless God breaks in, dooms us to live with the consequences: God's wrath.[1]

> By refusing to utter the one thing we have to say as sinners, our confession of sin, we have nothing at all to say before God or about God. By remaining silent at the wrong time, we are forced to remain completely silent. (2001, p. 145)

But this place of nothingness within the story of the gospel provides the place in which God acts. Jüngel writes: 'sinners can only be released from this state of speechlessness by the power of a resurrection' (2001, p. 134). In the gospel, death is not the end of the story. At the very point at which 'sinners' are unable to escape using their own resources and are doomed to play out the inevitable consequences, from that place of a nothingness God steps in to do what humans cannot do for themselves. He brings something out of nothing.

Justification is the restoration of these relationships from the point of nothingness. God is a God who speaks, through his Word, whom we learn in John's Gospel is Jesus Christ. He is a creative Word, who calls all things into existence out of nothing at the beginning (cf. Gen. 1; Rom. 4.17). The nature of the Word is to call life into being from nothingness (or death), through resurrection to new life (Jüngel, 2001, pp. 198–9).

The Word of God calls the believer away from themselves, away from their own solutions, in order to become themselves, through grace, by his righteousness. Jüngel claims that the sin we have is to want to find our own solutions by reaching inwards to ourselves, but these solutions can only take us to the place of relationlessness. We cannot rebuild the four directions of relationship on our own. Into this place, the creative Word speaks and calls us to understand and experience ourselves through the cross and resurrection, bringing renewal. This place of renewal is the act of justification, as God imparts his righteousness, restoring relationship and providing identity. Hence Paul declares: 'if anyone is in Christ, the new creation has come: the old has gone, the new is here!' (2 Cor. 5.17). As Jüngel writes:

> Jesus' resurrection from the dead promises that we shall be made anew out of the nothingness of relationlessness, remade *ex nihilo*, if through faith in the created Word of God we allow ourselves to participate in the love of God which occurs as the death of Jesus Christ. In this sense, Christian existence is existence out of nothingness, because it is all along the line existence out of the creative power of God who justifies. (1989, p. 108)

Justification is the whole sense of being restored to relationship with God and being made new in him.

Although this is not his aim, an understanding of church does emerge from Jüngel's in-depth theology. Following Luther, he understands the church as a community of the justified (2001, p. 222). Wherever there is a recognition of need for God, out of the place of nothingness, the church is (2001, p. 146). From this we could say that the church exists at the point of justification. He then applies the doctrine to some specific practices. Worship is to be about praise and thanksgiving to God by the community of the justified, those brought into a restored relationship with him (2001, p. 268). These communities must be places where everyone is valued. As God has declared there are no 'hopeless cases' in humanity but sees fit to justify everyone who comes to him, likewise the church must be a community for all (2001, p. 269). Jüngel also makes a case for extending the righteousness of God beyond the community to 'the stranger' (2001, p. 271). This could be seen as a basis for social justice, mission and evangelism. These represent the beginnings of an application from Jüngel, but he himself gets no more specific than that. More concrete applications based on his work are to come from practical theologians such as Andrew Root.

The place of encounter

Andrew Root comes from a background in youth ministry. It is therefore unsurprising that his theology is grounded on experience. His theology in *Christopraxis: A Practical Theology of the Cross*, rests on the assertion that God speaks and acts in the lives of ordinary people from places of nothingness, that these concrete and lived experiences of God are transformational, and they occur in the acts of ministering or in being ministered to.

Like Barth and Jüngel, Root's theological focus is on Jesus rather than the Trinity as a whole. The reason is because Root sees Jesus as the interpretative lens of God's ministry and the lens for understanding God. What we know about God we know through Jesus. Jesus is the image of the invisible God, supreme over creation. He holds everything together and is the exact representation of God's being (cf. Col. 1.15–17; Heb. 1.3). Therefore Jesus' work is not only the work of God but the way we see God working in the world. Root comes to his practical theology through Jüngel's justification.

In *Christopraxis* he describes some empirical research into the lived experiences among people from two congregations in the north-western states of the USA. Those interviewed were asked about their concrete experiences of God. They described their situations as being, metaphorically, at 'the end of a rope', 'in a hole' and 'at the end of themselves'. There was nothing they could do to affect the situation in which they found themselves. Borrowing from Jüngel, he calls these places of nothingness. For one the experience was related to the death of a

spouse; for another there was a sense of exasperation or pow-
erlessness at work. For others the experiences came out of the
practice of ministry. Through serving, they experienced God
in the work they were doing, through and in the people to
whom they were ministering. For each of them there was a
sense that they were fully reliant on God in that situation. They
had reached the end of their own solutions and needed God to
step in.

This is at the heart of Root's practical theology of the cross:
God operates through what from a human perspective appears
to be foolishness, choosing the unlikely or impossible in order
to achieve his ends. Where human means are at an end, God
acts. We can trace this pattern through Scripture. Abraham is
called, childless, at an old age and told he will be the father
to many nations. His son Isaac is the product of Sarah's old
and infertile womb. Isaac is chosen over Abraham's other son,
Ishmael, who was conceived with Abraham's slave Hagar
as a result of Abraham and Sarah taking matters into their
own hands, trying to hasten the fulfilment of God's promise.
Ishmael was born from human will, not God's action. Moses,
plucked from a life of shepherding in Midian with just a staff,
is empowered by God to lead the Hebrews against the might
of Pharaoh. Jesus too, born from a virgin's womb then handed
over to die at the hands of a mighty human empire, was raised
to new life. At each point in these and many other biblical
passages, God's possibility emerges from human impossibility. Extending this pattern of God acting at points of human
impossibility, Root contends that God makes himself known
when we've got to the end of ourselves; God acts *ex nihilo*,
out of nothing. He does this through his identification with
us in Christ, both fully human and fully God. And when God
does this, he brings life and new possibility. This, for Root, is
not only the place in which God acts but the place from which
ministry springs.

The framework for ministry, for Root, then becomes 'divine
possibility' – what can God do? Justification is an action of
God. The doctrine gives 'vision' to the action of God in human
experience, through God's action of ministry. He writes:

'justification encompasses the shape of divine action next to concrete human existence' (2014, p. 121). Justification is therefore, according to Root, how God deals with the world:

> Having been given life out of death, having encountered the new possibility in and through the perishing Jesus who now lives, we claim Christ as Lord, as sure God. We are moved to claim this God as the relationship of three in one by the concrete experience of God's being as becoming in the act of justification in and through Jesus (through the act of God's ministry itself). (2014, p. 122)

Justification is the point of God's possibility at our points of human impossibility: 'It is the beautiful yearning for new life next to concrete and lived experiences of impossibility, the impossibility of sick children, grieving friends, absent spouses, and soul-smothering jobs' (2014, p. 123). In these concrete situations, out of nothing, God speaks and restores. From the experience of God in this place we lose the need to be self-realizing or self-justifying. In being justified, by the grace of God we are made fully human. Christ brings to us a new experience; lives are redefined to become authentically human. Here Root's view of justification follows Jüngel's.

But Root goes further in that this is the place where ministry needs to begin, in the places of nothingness. Where Jüngel only touched on what justification could mean for the ministry of the church, Root spells out how the theory becomes praxis:

> Concrete and lived places of God's absence are the very places where ministry begins, for in these places of God's absence, places of nothingness and impossibility, the creative Word that has entered the cross and resurrection moves, bringing new possibility. (2014, p. 135)

As these are the places where God is at work, these are the places where ministry begins. The fresh expression saying of mission being 'finding out what God is doing and joining in' meets theology here. Ministry, therefore, is not dependent on the activity that we can create but on working out of the places of nothingness where God is already working. In sharing the experience of nothingness with others, we trust that when the event is shared, a connection with the eternal is made:

> When the suffering mother speaks of the son's mental illness, when a wife speaks of the death of her husband, or when the young man speaks of the stress of a dehumanizing job, the event of sharing is born as new possibility in and through nothingness. (2014, p. 136)

Ministry is participation in God's transformation from nothingness, from brokenness to new life.

This may appear to indicate that the Christian faith can only have something to say to people who are in places of crisis. I don't think this needs to be the case. While a point of crisis can undoubtedly be an experience of nothingness and the impetus to reach out to God, God can present experiences of new possibility even when those points of human impossibility have not yet been acknowledged. Through an encounter with Christ, God has something to say to those who would maintain a 'stiff upper lip', to those who would encourage people to 'reach deep inside themselves' to find their identity and solutions, or to those for whom life seems to be going well. Here the point of nothingness, or reaching the boundary of human limitation may not be acknowledged but it can be met all the same by an experience of transcendence from the all-knowing and loving God. I think of the man who described to me his encounter with Jesus during the course of an ordinary working day on the reception desk of a gym. There was no crisis point. He was not particularly searching for transcendence at that time. However, he would admit that his life has since been changed irrevocably. Likewise, Root describes two people he interviewed who experienced God through their practice of ministry, before they had necessarily reached their limitations (2014, pp. 44–5). Life is given extra purpose, a new vision, greater meaning through an atoning encounter with God in some way. The Christian faith can encourage people to reach outside of themselves even when there may be some 'human' possibility left to explore. This reaching out is creating space to experience transcendence and is the nothing place that God speaks into. However, God can speak into these spaces even when they are not acknowledged.

Root's theory arises out of and is concretely embedded in ministerial practice. This is the opposite direction of thought to that of Schmiechen and others outlined in the previous chapter. They have argued from theology to practice. Here ministry affects theology; the starting point is where God meets with humanity in everyday situations. Of course, Root, through Jüngel, has only spoken of justification. What about the other theories and images of atonement? They all indicate where and how God is at work, bringing all creation to himself. Starting from this point of encounter we can see other aspects of atonement being embodied in ministerial practice. We can then make a case for using these atonement theories to evaluate a fresh expression or even determine what some of the activities of a new contextual church should be. If God is at work at the point of nothingness, then justification, alongside sanctification, liberation, restoration and forgiveness, can be seen to be happening. In order to live out atonement and participate in God's work, the church must see the points at which God is to be found, meeting with people *ex nihilo* and creating spaces where they can open themselves up to God from a place of nothingness. Starting here makes the church cross-shaped.

What might this look like?

We have seen in the previous two chapters that different theological starting points and different atonement theories each causatively affect the form of the church and can inspire it to action in various ways. As the body of Christ, the church continues the work of Christ both as a witness to him and as a participant by the power of the Spirit. God's action through Christ is cross-shaped. Therefore it is not unreasonable to use the various theories of the doctrine of atonement to evaluate or determine the practices of a church. Many of the writers above have not dealt explicitly with the practices of the church – baptism, Eucharist, preaching and fellowship. These are certainly not irrelevant. Indeed, Scot McKnight argues that these practices, alongside prayer, are atoning (2007, pp. 144–54). They are essential to every church as they initiate, celebrate, remember, proclaim and live out the work of Christ. In the case of prayer, it connects the community to the living God. Eucharist centres our attention on the saving work of Christ. In baptism we initiate into the 'community of the justified'. But simply, whether they are or are not in evidence does not determine the success or quality of church that is found in a particular place. I would expect contextual questions to be asked about how they are being practised and how they are being received. Focusing on atonement, however, centres on the work of Christ in all of the practices of the church, resulting in a variety of forms of church that can arise. The question one should ask regarding fresh expressions or indeed any church might be, using a broad definition of atonement: 'Are people being atoned'? This question gives us a starting point from which one can evaluate whether a fresh expression is doing the work of the kingdom. It could also be used to guide practices that may be initiated. In starting a new ecclesial community, attention might be given to developing practices that allow space for God to be at work; or in other words, places where atonement can occur. These would look different according to the context in which the new ecclesial community is working, but drawing the rationale for the practices and ministries of a church from an understanding of how God is at work in the world through Christ enables a church to be truly cross-shaped.

Regarding justification, one might ask whether people are receiving the righteousness of God. Are they being brought to an experience of the goodness of God? Can they embody and inhabit their new identity living within the possibility of God? This may take place through an inner conviction, through preaching or Bible study. It may take place in the margins by searching out those lost and broken souls who are struggling with life. It may take place in a small group with honest and accountable trust. It might be a group of young people who, as they discover what God's righteousness imparted to them means for their identity, open themselves up to explore the calling of God's possibility on their lives, confident they no longer need to construct their identity using human means.

If God meets people in the place of nothingness, we might ask whether the church is actively looking for the places of nothingness around them. Is the body of Christ being the presence of Christ in those places? That God meets people at the point of nothingness surely offers a reason for the church to intentionally place itself in the heart of the community. The pioneer's first inclination is usually to spend time hanging out, building relationships. By spending time in the places where people gather, whether that is the local pub, coffee shop, skate park or sports club, Christians, as the dispersed body of Christ, take Christ out into the community. It is not that he is not already there, but they can point, guide and direct towards God's all-embracing justification. In the community they are able to build relationships and hear stories. They can share in the joys and sorrows of others and, perhaps, offer God's love and truth into their struggles and vulnerabilities as personal nothing-places are articulated and shared.

Regarding reconciliation, is the community reconciled and united with one another? Are people brought into reconciled relationships with God and are there opportunities for relationships to be repaired in the church and through the church? Here the church would be providing opportunities to confess and receive forgiveness from God. They may also provide some reconciliation resources themselves, or signpost to externally run mediation services. Within the church, a reconciled community would promote honest and accountable relationships, providing spaces for people to share their stories of guilt and shame without fear of human condemnation. Each of these also starts from the realization that reconciliation, both with God and with others, cannot come about through human effort alone – a place of nothingness. It is the cross that enables forgiveness to be received from God, and the Holy Spirit who enables us to forgive others.

From a sanctification image of atonement we could ask whether people are becoming more holy. Are people being transformed? Is there a change in their living patterns? Whether this is happening comes down to whether the church is providing opportunities for discipleship. While the example theory, which as I noted in the previous chapter is not really a theory of atonement, offers Jesus as a model for Christian life, sanctification through atonement recognizes that God needs to step in and effect change. After the cross and resurrection, Jesus gave his Holy Spirit. In order to grow in faith and holiness, there must be a realization of the need for change. Much of this is personal but it can be encouraged and supported in the community of a congregation.

Henri Nouwen recognizes the importance of discipline and the contemplative aspect in personal prayer. He claims that transformation comes through three aspects of spiritual disciplines: the church, the Word and the heart. These roughly equate to partaking in a rhythm of prayer in community throughout the liturgical year, having a focus on meditation on Scripture, and a commitment to personal prayer (2007, pp. 69ff.). Regarding personal prayer, he writes: 'entering into the solitude of our closet and standing there with nothing but our own nakedness, vulnerability, and sinfulness, requires an intense commitment to the spiritual life' (2007, p. 83). This 'enables us to cry out for the unconditional mercy of God' (2007, p. 87). Here he recognizes that Christian discipleship requires a commitment to seek out those places of nothingness in our lives that we would rather ignore or cover up with busyness. In fresh expressions one cannot expect this level of commitment from the previously unchurched from day one, but a culture modelling what such a lifestyle might look like can be created. Commitment to the spiritual life in this way can be modelled and encouraged through small groups. Those communities that adhere to a rule of life, such as new monastic communities, may have an advantage here.

But personal transformation through discipleship can take many forms. In Messy Churches – which do not usually adhere to a common rule of life like new monastic communities – the question of discipleship has been an ongoing concern. Paul Moore, the vicar of the parish church in Cowplain,

Hampshire where the first Messy Church was created, encourages churches to think about discipleship occurring in three ways: formal, non-formal and socialization (2013, pp. 36–40). Churches concerned about sanctification through discipleship might engage in formal intentional teaching through upfront input, courses, group study or discussion. They might also create opportunities for non-formal learning to happen as new or younger Christians engage in acts of service alongside someone who has being doing it for longer. Finally, simply the act of being in a culture where personal holiness and transformation are taken seriously enables others in the environment to pick up some of those values naturally, by osmosis. This is how children learn language and values from their families. Moore goes on to argue that all three of these aspects to discipleship can be seen in the Bible. These values could clearly be applied in other forms of contextual church. In providing avenues for deepening discipleship, a fresh expression is participating in the sanctifying action of God through Christ, one of the ongoing aspects of atonement. They are creating space for people to open themselves up to him and allow God's process of sanctification to occur.

From the *Christus Victor* theory, the victory motif prompts us to ask whether Christians are experiencing freedom from whatever binds them, be it addictions, ways of thinking, unjust structures or patterns of living. Again, these will be different in each context. In some cases it may be appropriate to offer courses that help people to overcome addictions or to signpost people into the Christian programmes that exist. In a professional environment the powers in play may be corporate expectations to be giving the best of oneself to the company and to be forever climbing the career ladder, perhaps at the expense of family or mental health. An atonement community can offer an alternative way, in which although success is valued and celebrated, it is not seen as the goal of life. Diversity in church can help here too, as corporate professionals are brought alongside, say, single mums who work only for the benefit of their families, or disabled children whose value lies not in what they can contribute to the world but in who they are. A *Christus Victor* community is one in which everyone is welcome and valued.

At the same time, *Christus Victor* also prompts us to ask whether the community is living as a community defined by the victory of God. Is there a distinction between the way the Christian community approaches the ethical, economic, social or political sphere, and the way these things are dealt with by wider society? As Driver notes, the Church is a participant in the cosmic role of restoration that Jesus effects through the presence of the Holy Spirit (1986, p. 233). Fresh expressions, like all churches, will be playing their part in combatting injustice and therefore spreading justice (righteousness) and peace. This may involve combatting poverty by hosting or contributing to a foodbank, offering a space for advice or legal services to the under-represented, or promoting godly stewardship of the environment.

We could do the same for the other images of atonement. Regarding Christ's sacrifice, we may ask whether fresh expressions are demonstrating self-giving love to the world and are involved in areas where incarnational mission is a sacrifice. And concerning substitution, are churches demonstrating grace to the outsider? While there is surely overlap between the different images, taking even just a few of them allows us to assess where God is in the work of the church. None of them are prescriptive about church practices or style. In this way, using atonement as a guiding doctrine for ecclesiology enables the church to be contextual while also ensuring that the essential elements of salvation are evident in the shape of church – that the church is cross-shaped. All of the images of atonement applied in this way witness to the reign of Christ in the world. To be sure, there are no easy answers to what these actions will look like or whether they are in evidence in a fresh expression. But this starting point allows us to tell and hear the stories of where God is at work, and to judge the work of the church on that rather than on practices or statistics.

The first DVD collection of stories from Fresh Expressions contains the story of Zac's Place, a fresh expression that met in a bar and offered a space for those from the artistic community, the biker community and those on the fringes of society to engage with God. It began to attract people who the pastor, Sean Stillman, described as 'ragamuffins'. Near the end of the piece, Sean relates a story of a homeless young lady with addictions who came in one evening, highly strung and foul-mouthed, disrupting the meeting. She was very agitated. While some were trying to calm her down, one of the members departed and came back with a basin of warm water and proceeded to wash her feet. Sean remarked: 'I have never seen someone's demeanour change so quickly. She had gone from being foul-mouthed and abusive, to sitting back in her chair, relaxing, and singing "Jesus Loves Me, This I Know."' A week later she was found to have died from an overdose, but in that moment she experienced something of the love of God for her and was able to express it in the simple song she had known as a child.[2] Certainly this one instance alone doesn't make Zac's Place a church, but it indicates that they are doing the work of church. Through her experience, in her place of nothingness, the young lady was able to experience the love God had for her and the value he places on her. She was accepted into a community of faith, and she turned this into praise. In it she experienced atonement. Surely other such stories can be unearthed and used to evaluate a fresh expression through the experience of atonement in a way that can be so much more instructive than simply looking at numbers or practices. This is what I will turn to next. After exploring the difficulties of evaluating a new ecclesial community in terms of numbers or through the idea of sustainability, in the final chapter I share some stories from the life of Berrywood Church that demonstrate how the church was participating in the atoning actions of God occurring through its ministries and the day-to-day lives of its members.

Notes

1 Jüngel conceives of God's wrath not as a separate action of God but as the antithesis of the imparting of God's righteousness. Wrath is simply the consequences of human sin played out (2001, pp. 66–9).

2 'Zac's Place', *Expressions: Making a Difference* (DVD) (Fresh Expressions, 2011), ch. 28.

7

What is success?

Before starting our pioneering venture in Northampton, had someone told me that by the end of my stay, the resulting church would have only 35 regular attendees at the worship gathering, and those only when everyone turned up in the same week, I would have been disappointed. I had expected to see a growing network of activities across the community, which was happening, but I had also hoped that a significant number would be attending a worship gathering and coming to faith. As we started, I had assumed our gathering would be in the community centre on the St Crispin's development, which was due to be built within the first 18 months of my post. In fact building only began in the month we were preparing to leave. The delay on this centre meant that the worship gathering met in a location away from the development for most of our time. My expectations also reflected my subconscious and unexamined – but incorrect – assumption that a growing church is a measure of successful corporate discipleship. These expectations gradually changed over the five years as I began to appreciate the deeper things going on in people's lives, regardless of numbers. Berrywood Church was small, and that was okay.

But still the project needed to be evaluated, both for the sake of forward planning in Duston and for the wider strategic vision of the diocese. The last of my four project milestones, to which I was held accountable by a steering group, had called for sustainability, which, while it was never indicated what shape of church should emerge, focused on discipleship, leadership and finance. The evaluation questions supplied by the steering group to determine whether the objectives of this milestone were being met placed emphasis on the financial security, vision and the passing on of leadership (see Withington, 2011). They also mentioned the three-self principle of the nineteenth-century mission strategist Henry Venn: that a church should be self-governing, self-financing and self-reproducing. These were joined by a fourth 'self', self-theologizing, added by Paul Hiebert in the 1980s.

Is this concept of sustainability a useful one with which to evaluate a new contextual church? Are questions of size, governance, leadership, finance and discipleship the right tools to use? In this final chapter I will address these questions, including those raised by the three-self principle, and argue that the cross-shaped approach offers a useful theological lens through which to ask evaluative questions of a new ecclesial community.

Is small beautiful?

By the end of my time, five years into the post and just over three years since we had started worshipping together, the numerical statistics indicated that we had 35 regular attendees at our worship gatherings. Of course, our reach into the community went much further than that, numbering in the hundreds, but for the moment I will consider only those who attended worship, to help us think about the difficulties of defining church through Sunday attendees. In the initial core team there were seven adults (and five children), two of whom were fringe attendees at other churches before they joined with us. In the first year, when we were still meeting once a month, we grew to have 16 adults and 12 children whom I would consider regulars (this number excludes people who only attended once). This demonstrates over 100 per cent growth in numbers in the first year, most of the growth coming from those who did not previously attend church. Over the following two years this number of regulars grew slightly, to include about 20 adults and 15 children. Even though we increased the number of weekly worship services so that those who came now had the option of coming three times a month, numerical growth slowed dramatically from the fast start we had experienced. At the time, I wrote on my blog:

> Being honest, five years ago I might have hoped for the numbers to be higher by this point, but we rejoice that of our 20 adults, about half have either come to faith, or are on the journey, and others have grown in faith immensely since they joined us. (Dunlop, 2015)

Clearly things were happening, but they had not resulted in large numbers coming to gather at our main worship services.

Regarding size, small is not unusual when it comes to new ecclesial communities. Church Army research into fresh expressions across half the dioceses of the Church of England found that most are small, 64 per cent having fewer than 50 attendees (Lings, 2016, p. 39). Only 9 per cent have over 100 people attending, while only 2 per cent have over 200. This latter figure may be down to the researcher's decision to include HTB-style resource church plants in his definition of fresh expressions, but he adds that there is no suggestion that these larger fresh expressions attract a greater proportion of outsiders to the church.[1] Lings argues that small is the norm, and small can be effective. The Church Army named their report *The Day of Small Things* in response to these findings, as they envisaged the future of a network of small communities, each reaching into many different aspects of society.

Regarding growth, Lings' research team noted that it is a mistake to think that all fresh expressions keep on growing. Although many do, nearly half reach a numerical plateau, as we appeared to have done, while nearly a quarter grow then shrink. Some cease altogether, due either to their outlasting their original purpose, failing to gain traction or, often, losing momentum on the departure of the original leader. At the launch presentation of this data, Lings remarked that it is 'not good to say that everything that is healthy gets bigger. With things that are organic, this is not true. Shallots do not become onions. But they do multiply.'[2] It is worth noting that in the book of Acts, besides a couple of occasions when large numbers of people converted (such as at Pentecost), the descriptions of early churches indicate that most were small. But they did multiply, as members were sent off to found new small ecclesial communities in other parts of the city or in other towns and villages. Their intention was to multiply.

The resulting landscape of many small new ecclesial communities is one that may be able to adapt more quickly than large organizations to changes in contemporary culture. Through many small contextual communities, the Church is then able to be truly local in a way that a geographical parish may struggle to be. Each small ecclesial community, which may be located in a workplace, sports club, community hall or home, can then contextualize to the shape of the community of people it is trying to serve.

How should we evaluate sustainability?

If size is not a useful measure of evaluating the success of a fresh expression venture, many have turned to the idea of sustainability. As I stated above, my project had specific questions by which to begin discussing sustainability, which were set out as project milestones and evaluation questions alongside the role description. They focused on financial security, vision and the passing on of leadership. These evaluation questions were inspired by the work of Henry Venn and the development of his principles by Paul Hiebert.

Venn was an Anglican clergyman, missioner and social activist of the nineteenth century who was involved with the Church Mission Society for many years. In the course of his work there, dealing mainly with overseas mission, he developed the three-self principle as a tool to judge the state of the church in a new location. His desire was to see faith communities able to resource themselves, both financially and in terms of leadership and decision-making, independently of the mission agency (self-governing, self-financing). In time they would also be self-reproducing, engaging in mission in their area and starting new churches. One hundred years later the missiologist

Paul Hiebert added a fourth 'self', self-theologizing, which can be fulfilled when a church in a location is able to read and interpret Scripture for their own culture (Hiebert, 1985, pp. 195ff.). This allows for elements of contextualization in a church. This fourth principle can clearly be seen in Vincent Donovan's approach to bringing Christianity to the Masai people of Tanzania in the 1960s, although he himself does not name it as such (Donovan, 1982).

Can these four 'selves' be useful to new ecclesial communities today? The situation for fresh expressions is complicated. Self-government might be difficult for many. Some will always be linked to a founding church, such as many Messy Church congregations whose leadership and financing continue to come from the sending church. Other new ecclesial communities will struggle with becoming self-financing. For example, youth congregations cannot be expected to fully fund a paid youth worker themselves. However, it is worth noting that even among traditional congregations in the Anglican Church, the four selves are not always fulfilled: there are many who share their governance with neighbouring churches, are not able to pay for their own minister and maintenance, or have no desire to reproduce themselves.

Moynagh (2012, p. 406) suggests that for new ecclesial communities, the four-self principle could be understood more radically, judging what is the most appropriate form of each 'self' for the congregation in question. For example, a youth congregation could be regarded as self-financing if the youth worker has access to funds to cover his or her own costs, either through a community initiative, regular source of funding or part-time work. A church could be regarded as self-governing if it has appropriate independence in making its own decisions, even though it may share administrative or leadership resources with other churches.

At Berrywood we were certainly not self-financing, as we were still relying on some of the budget provided by the diocese, but through the giving of members of the congregation (mostly the core team), we were moving in that direction. Our governance was mostly independent, although I was accountable to the steering group overseeing the project. We were also reaching out to our community in mission and starting up new initiatives, so it could also be argued that we were self-reproducing.

However, I'm still unconvinced as to the helpfulness of the four-self approach. Regarding sustainability, the 'selves' can tell us lots about the structure of the church and the organization of it, and remarkably little about the relationships within the church, or the relationships the church has with others. While our culture raises up the concept of independence as a virtue, for churches, *inter*dependence may be a better one, as it highlights this value of relationship. It is also possible to fulfil the four selves yet be ineffective in many ways. For example, Moynagh adds that a church could fulfil the four selves but at the same time fail to be contextual, simply reproducing new versions of itself (2017, p. 375).

The four selves could also be open to abuse. In China the state-run church that was founded in the 1950s named itself the Three-Self Patriotic Movement after these principles (before the fourth 'self' was added). This followed many years of foreign-led mission activity in China that adopted Venn's three-self principle in order to aid indigenization and enculturation of the Church in that context. While the Three-Self Patriotic Movement is based on and fulfils the criteria of the three-self principle, it is also heavily tied to the politics of the government, which limits what can and cannot be said and done. I argued in the last chapter about church being relational, based on how God is at work in the world and in the lives of individuals and communities. The four selves have the disadvantage of focusing on structure rather than relationships.

Seeing these difficulties in the four-self principle, in *Church for Every Context*, Moynagh attempts to find a more suitable construct for discussing sustainability (2012, pp. 406–8). He summarizes categories for analysing sustainability under four headings (which all usefully begin with an 'f'). First, is the initiative bearing *fruit* in that people are coming to explore faith and moving deeper in their journey with Christ? Second, is it paying attention to the *flow* of people? When a member moves away, moves beyond the intended demographic of the new ecclesial community, or simply wants to seek a different style of worship, are they being helped into another more appropriate community? Third, is the new contextual church connected to the wider church *family* in a denomination or network? And fourth, does it have an appropriate level of *freedom* in making decisions? The word 'appropriate' arises from his discussion of the four selves above. These are undoubtedly useful concepts, moving the discussion of sustainability on from financials, numbers, structure and converts, to focus on relationship.

However, in his more recent book, *Church in Life*, Moynagh has radically rethought his four 'f's. Here he questions the whole idea of sustainability itself: 'What matters is not the durability of new ecclesial communities, but their fruitfulness . . . It is not difficult to think of congregations that have existed for many years but no longer appear fruitful' (2017, p. 375). Simple longevity is not the aim for any church. The aim is to bear fruit. This focuses the question on what is happening in terms of relationships, discipleship and individual journeys, rather than structures or finance. We then need to ask what fruitfulness in a new ecclesial community might look like, especially given the diversity of shapes that such communities can take.

So how might one measure fruitfulness? One solution, which Moynagh follows, is to revert to the four directions of relationship – *up*, *in*, *out* and *of* – as a guide for assessment (2017, p. 377). This is one of the potential distilled ecclesiologies I mentioned in Chapter 3. This framework can then be applied at each stage of the serving-first journey (see Figure 1 in Chapter 1) to assess whether the appropriate fruit has been borne for that stage of the church's development. At periodic intervals, reviews look back over the previous stage and then assess what might be appropriate fruit for the next stage. For example, instead of setting out a timescale for progress as my milestones had done, reviews could commit to evaluating fruitfulness according to which stage of the serving-first journey the pioneering team is currently working in. While my milestones allocated six months for mapping the context and building relationships, there may be places where a much longer period of time is required, especially in cases where there is a cultural barrier to overcome. In some deprived areas, residents are used to government initiatives that promise much but are then withdrawn a couple of years later. They can be wary of new promises. In such a context it may be that, say, a middle-class pioneer has to work at building relationships for up to two years to overcome suspicions before trust is built up. During this period, in the 'active listening' stage of the serving-first journey, fruitfulness can only helpfully be evaluated in terms of depth of relationships that have been formed.

As fruitfulness is based on the four directions of relationship, it can also be seen as cross-shaped. The four directions focus our attention *up* with God, *in* with one another, *out* to the world and *of* the wider church. These align almost exactly with the four directions of relationship that were ruptured at the fall and repaired through Christ's atoning work. Likewise, the concept of fruit is always linked to God's action. It is God's action that affects our relationships with him, with others, with the church and with the world. As Jesus says in John's Gospel: 'If you remain in me and I in you, you will bear much fruit; apart from me you can do nothing' (John 15.5). Bearing fruit is inextricably related to God's action through Jesus. I am arguing that these four directions of relationship can been seen in the primary action of God through Jesus, in the atonement. Therefore the key question to ask when thinking about the evaluation or fruitfulness of a new ecclesial community, is: 'Are people being atoned?'

Atonement and fruitfulness

In the last chapter I described how God meets us at places of nothingness, at the end of human limitations, even if those limitations have not yet been acknowledged. These places of encounter are atoning moments when God reaches out to us and draws us in to himself. If, as I have argued, the Church is to witness to and participate in the action of God through Christ, we can therefore use the doctrine of atonement in our shaping of and evaluation of new ecclesial communities. This ensures that our churches remain cross-shaped, focused on the

essential work of God in the world. This approach is inher-
ently relational and pays attention to the four directions of
relationships that exist – with God, with others in the community, with the world and with the wider Church (*up, in, out*
and *of*). Atonement also affects our self-understanding as we
come to find our identity in Christ and to see ourselves as God,
through Christ, sees us. In this regard it adds a fifth direction:
relationship with ourselves. The effects of Christ's justification,
sanctification, victory and other aspects of atonement flow out
into all our relationships, into the Church and into our own
self-understanding.

I also outlined in the previous chapter how different aspects
of the atonement might play out in the ministries of the Church.
How did we see this happening in Berrywood? I will share a
few examples.

First, at around a year into our post I remember sitting in
our back garden on a sunny Friday morning with the mums
who had started to gather to read the Bible and pray. At this
point it was a fairly small group of us. I think there were just
me, Kate, Laura and Helen, the latter two having just had their
babies. My wife, Sarah, was away that day. In many ways,
as a group we were still getting to know each another. I cannot remember the passage we were studying but I do remember that this was the first time Helen shared openly about her
clinical anxiety. She explained how it makes her feel, how she
has to spend time away from people and how she treads a
delicate balance of medication. Unknown to Helen, the effect
of this admission, which came from a point of weakness or
vulnerability in her, was to allow space in the group for God
to speak into our limitations, anxieties and weaknesses. It set
a precedent for the group to become a place of honesty and
openness, where anything could be shared and where members
did not have to put on their best appearance to each other
when they came together. We became able to share anything
that was concerning us, regardless of how large or insignificant
it might appear. If it was a concern then it could be aired and
the group would pray. There are elements of *Christus Victor*
here – Christ's victory over all that oppresses – as the group

became aware of God's interest in the realities of our lives and the freedom he gives through Christ. There are also aspects of reconciliation with God as issues were named and brought before God.

A second example came from the community. In the first six months I had intentionally spent time in the community, and part of this included joining the residents' association. This had been formed just a few months before we arrived in St Crispin's, initially in reaction to the developer's decision to build 80 more houses, which were not in the original plans, before essential infrastructure work was complete. At the time of forming the group out of this reactionary impetus, the residents decided that the association could also offer important community-building events. This was where I saw that I could be most useful, so I joined the social committee subgroup. After an initial summer bank-holiday picnic and then a more ambitious fireworks evening to celebrate St Crispin's day in October, the social committee began discussing whether to do anything over Christmas. A few ideas were shared. I had expected us to settle on some form of outdoor carol singing, perhaps with a Christmas tree and a band from the local Salvation Army. However, the suggestion came from within the group to have a Christingle service, as members had remembered enjoying them as children. Now, I am not a great fan of the Christingle as a mechanism for explaining the gospel. During the first Christmas of my curacy, faced with attending one for the first time in many years (and having to lead it!), while I could remember that the light was Jesus, I had to remind myself what the orange, sticks, nuts, sweets and ribbon of the Christingle stood for. This was despite having attended many Christingle services myself as a child. I had arrived in Northampton expecting (hoping?) never to have to do one again!

However, as this very Christian service was suggested from within the community as one of the ways they wanted to celebrate Christmas, I certainly wasn't going to oppose it. While I did not suggest it, I don't think the idea would have been shared had I not been physically present – in my clerical collar – in the room. They wanted God, in some form, in their Christmas. It gave a natural opportunity to sing Christian carols and share something of the good news of Jesus in his incarnation. In the centre of the estate stood the old hospital chapel building, now owned by the regional Greek Orthodox congregation and used every other Sunday. Inside, the delightful murals, which remained on the walls from its hospital days, were now on display alongside free-standing orthodox icons. The building would not have been suitable for the café-style services we ended up creating in our regular gatherings, but it was ideal for the more structured format of a Christingle service. Permission was sought and the service went ahead. That first year we nearly filled the building. It seemed that local people on our housing development really wanted to celebrate Christmas – and to acknowledge God in it – in their local community.

By the following year the residents' association was suffering from leadership issues and the number of active participants had diminished radically. However, as the Christingle was such as positive experience in the first year, we teamed up with Forefront Church and with willing members of the residents' association to put it on again. In the years that followed there was standing room only. People came to expect it and were happy to volunteer their time making the Christingles or serving refreshments. In our final year on St Crispin's, one lady, not knowing of our involvement in the service, explained to my wife how she had 'always' attended and would not have dreamt of missing it. For some it was the focal point of the Christmas celebration. They planned their celebration around it and invited different generations of their family. It became part of the pattern of Christmas celebrations in St Crispin's during our time there, and still continues today.

This could be seen as evidence of sanctification in the culture of the housing development, during the initial listening phase of the serving-first journey. The impetus for this Christian service of worship at Christmas came from the community, and they were eager to adopt it as their own. My presence as the community vicar enabled them to voice their desire for God in their Christmas celebrations. This was only an initial and subtle transformation in the culture, but I believe it illustrates the journey towards holiness that takes place through the sanctification aspect of atonement.

Elsewhere too – coming to my third example – my presence in the community could be seen as an impetus to transformation. About 50 metres up the street from our house stood the Northamptonshire Country Centre, an independent organization that had existed since the days of the old St Crispin's Hospital as a day centre to offer horticultural experience to those with learning difficulties. The development had been built around it. Due to changes in the way their funding was received, they were in a period of transition, with many uncertainties ahead. Sarah and I had first popped in shortly after we moved in, to buy some locally grown vegetables. Very soon afterwards the Centre approached me to ask whether I would consider being a trustee. I agreed and, alongside the rest of the board, we undertook many difficult conversations about the direction of the organization. As I was now a trustee I wanted to understand some of the day-to-day goings on, so I decided to pop into the Centre more regularly – every two or three weeks, getting to know the clients and staff. After about a year the chairman of the board approached me and asked whether I would consider being the chaplain to the Centre, which resulted in my making a point of attending each week. It could be argued that this, suggested by the non-church-going leader at the Centre, shows a willingness to bring God into everyday life. He recognized that perhaps there was something a Christian presence could offer to the lives of the staff and clients that went beyond the excellent service the staff were able to offer. It could be argued that this admission may have stemmed from a realization of human weakness, limitation or nothingness. Like the example above, this could also be seen as a step in the sanctification of the culture.

There is a fourth example, or incident, that sticks in my mind, which came about as a result of this chaplaincy. About a couple of years into it I was asked by one of my fellow trustees to take the funeral of his wife, who had died suddenly. They had two children, now in their forties, one of whom was a client of the Centre, although both had fairly severe learning difficulties. I remember spending quite some time with the widowed husband before the funeral, listening to stories of his life, their joys and struggles in raising two disabled children, the sacrifices they had made and his worries for their future now that he was getting older. The telling of that story – I'm not sure he had ever verbalized it in that way before – was a deeply spiritual moment in which God's healing and restoring presence was tangibly ministering to this man in his grief. This was his point of nothingness. It illustrates how the place of encounter at a point of human impossibility can be seen as a starting point for God's justification. God was beginning to restore the relationship and point towards the possibility of new life through and out of his grief.

Experiencing reconciliation

The examples above offer some insight into how atonement can be seen in the everyday ministries of a new ecclesial community, although they could equally have been drawn from the ministry of a more traditional congregation. They are only snapshots – anecdotal stories told from the perspective of the minister rather than those experiencing the ministry. However, one former member of the Berrywood community was gracious enough to allow me to interview her about her experiences during the two-year period she was living on the St Crispin's development. This interview and the experiences of atonement that are revealed give a deeper picture of what God was doing in her life than the anecdotal stories above allow.

  When she arrived in July 2012, Jenny was a full-time mum and pregnant with her second child. She did not drive. She moved to the St Crispin's estate with her husband, Chris, who was a lower-league footballer recently transferred to a nearby team. They spent two years living on our street before Chris returned to the team he had come from in the North East, as a result of which they moved away. Jenny is bright, intelligent, outgoing and friendly, yet her initial experience of making friends in a new place was difficult. Her story is an experience of reconciliation with others, with God and with herself. I share some of this story in her own words.

First, she experiences a journey from isolation to support, bringing her back into human community. She had not wanted to move and initially felt very alone:

> We moved there for his job. Obviously I was technically on maternity leave already, so it's not like I was meeting anyone through work which is what I would have ordinarily done. I'd not got a baby yet so going to mother and baby groups wasn't really an option. I was just a pregnant woman with a toddler. We'd got him into nursery, which was great, but again, it wasn't the sort of nursery where you were interacting with other mums and stuff. It wasn't like waiting at the school gates, it was a private drop-off nursery and 'off you go', so I didn't really have a chance to meet anybody and talk with them.

Her sense of isolation was exacerbated by the design of the development. On St Crispin's, much of the allocated car parking was at the back of the houses. Instead of coming out the front door where they might bump into other residents, creating a neighbourly atmosphere, residents often left from the back of their houses, getting straight into their cars.

Jenny's inability to drive hindered her from getting around to local groups that were beyond walking distance, where she might otherwise have begun to make friends. Public transport options were also limited:

> Once Zak [my second son] was born I started venturing out a little bit more, going to, like, sensory rooms and things like that but even that I found quite hard to try and . . . it were quite spread out, Northampton, so it was hard, and being in a new-build estate it was harder to know where everything is. I wasn't driving, everywhere was quite hard to get around, one bus an hour is kind of difficult. I spent a lot of time just by myself walking to different places.

She then articulated the effect this had on her:

> For the first year that I was in Northampton, I hated it, I wanted to come home. I wanted to come back to the North

East. I didn't want to stay there. Yeah, and I was just really, I was unhappy about being there, I just felt a bit lost, a bit lonely and isolated. I think I got quite withdrawn and I just seemed to spend a lot of time by myself and I think I spent an awful lot of money! Because I think it were just trying to fill gaps, so 'Oh well, I'll go to town, or . . .'

The lack of community and poor transport links resulted in her feeling isolated and being withdrawn from others. Later she uses the phrase 'stir crazy'. It had an effect on spending as she sought to make up for lack of interaction.

The turning point came in a chance meeting with me in the local play park. Her oldest son was the same age as my son, and as they played together I got chatting. At the end of our conversation in the play park, I casually mentioned my role in the community and the craft group, Sticky Fingers, that we ran in the local coffee shop, about 15 minutes' walk from her house. Through that she started to make some connections in the church and in the local community. A couple of months later she rang me up out of the blue, wanting to be made aware of everything else we did. Having enjoyed making initial connections, she wanted to get to know people more deeply, so began attending many of our other groups:

Everything just kind of all happened at once but yeah, I guess it just took that introduction from you at the park to know that you were kind of like there and in the vicinity and then, kind of like a stone's throw away there were all these people with all these kids who were all just so welcoming and just nice to be around and there was no . . . you know, I could roll up in jeans and like a hoodie with no make-up on and unwashed hair and nobody cared and it was nice to think that I could be having a horrible day and somebody down the street would just be there like 'If you need anything?' You know it was nice to just know you'd got someone, if the kids weren't very well.

In this extract we see, metaphorically, scales falling from her eyes as she discovered that close community was right there on her doorstep. She realized that she was not alone. Her words are significant: in that community she experienced acceptance, no judgement, and support. Through the craft group, her first experience was one of unconditional welcome in a non-threatening environment. By the end of her time, her experience was one of real deep friendship offering genuine concern and support. She was no longer alone. This transformation of her community experience also changed her perceptions of Northampton:

> . . . and to say that [at the beginning] it was a place that I couldn't wait to get out of, it's the only place that I ever was sad to leave!

Our small Christian community became a place of reconciliation from her nothingness of human isolation as she experienced the warmth of human welcome shown through Christian love.

The second journey Jenny went on was one of reconciliation with God. She did have a childhood faith, which was shared in her family only by her grandmother and an uncle. She remembers accompanying her grandma to church as a child, but the experiences were mostly negative. There was a sense of obligation, with expectations to learn the basis of faith through formal study, including sitting and passing exams. She remembers the building being old and not well heated. The services contained no interaction and she describes a 'judgemental' atmosphere. Despite this mostly negative experience, in several places in the interview she articulated that something was missing from her life, which she later discovered was this dormant faith.

But her positive experience of the wider Berrywood community overcame these negative associations of church. She describes that the next step, coming to church, was:

> . . . just like a natural progression. Once I'd been around everybody and saw how everybody interacted it just seemed like a natural progression to want to be back involved.

Her experience in the church community was one of welcome and acceptance, drawing her, quite easily, to make the leap to coming to our café-style gatherings. She particularly enjoyed the heavily interactive style of services. This resulted in a change in the way her faith played out in her everyday life, as well as growing trust in God, which also affected her identity (which will be discussed below). This journey continued after she moved away.

Jenny: I found community and family and faith at Berrywood. And I think that just stayed with me. And I still feel part of that community, and obviously I still have my faith [since she moved away], which I didn't have as strongly before. I certainly didn't feel right, you know, sitting at home and while [Chris] was in bed next to me, picking up my Bible and reading little bits . . .
Me: But you do that now?
Jenny: Yeah! Um. You know, the Bibles are always around, and they're on the desk, and they're next to the bed and stuff, and like I said, Zak picks it up and carries it around and Chris will say: 'Jen, can you pick that up and put that somewhere safe, because he's gonna damage it', or . . . so no, it's just like a normal [thing], you know, like leaving your hairbrush lying around.

This change in behaviour reflects the way her faith became integral to her sense of identity. This gradual process of discipleship over the course of the year she was at Berrywood came primarily through her involvement in the close-knit Friday-morning women's Bible group, but her regular attendance and involvement in our worship gatherings and all-age services would have had an effect too. During this time she purchased her own Bible and sought advice on how to read it and pray at home. This coming back to her faith could be regarded as an ongoing journey of reconciliation to God.

Third, Jenny experienced a form of reconciliation to herself as she began to find her own identity. Before coming into contact with Berrywood Church she described herself as rudderless, living vicariously through her husband, just waiting for him to get home each day, with no clear goals of her own. She didn't like who she was becoming:

> It created a lot of tension and it made me quite snappy and I didn't have anything else to do with my time . . . I didn't really have any direction, you know, even, you know, what I wanted to be or what I wanted to do, and I just kind of waited for him to come home every day, I was just this typical old-fashioned wife/mother staying at home and waiting to cook dinner and making cakes . . .

The transformation was partly due to the experience of community and partly to the re-finding of her faith. Looking back on her self-identity after having being involved in this community, she describes herself using very different words from before, and is almost surprised at how self-confident she has become:

> [My faith] just seemed to give me a lot more . . . a lot more self-confidence in myself, and just kind of stop worrying, I don't know it's really strange. Especially now I can find myself sitting thinking 'How am I coping?' [. . .] I'm not worrying about whether Chris is going to get another contract, or [anything else] because I just think, it's going to work out, because now I've just got the faith to know that it will work out the way that it's supposed to, and if now is not the right time for me to go to Uni then I think there's a reason because it's not the right time and I'll just roll with it. And I think it just gives me a lot more, er, comfort. Before I struggled a lot with anxiety and depression.

In her words, the Berrywood community helped her become more self-confident, self-assured, secure in herself, and gave her a strong sense of purpose. It even improved her mental health. Again, in the extract below we see her change in self-perception fuelled by her faith:

Now I feel like this amazing indestructible amazing woman and I can do anything that I want to do, and kind of like, you know, there's not . . . I feel like, lately, there's nothing that I can't do. So, which is strange going from leaving home at 19 and kind of just following Chris around the country [. . .] I was just rolling with it and seeing what was gonna happen, whereas now I've got like, some driving force behind me and some kind of spurring on.

Since leaving Northampton they have been settled and static in the North East for a few years. Jenny has had the confidence – and the support from her husband – to develop her own ambitions and take steps towards fulfilling them. As a mature student, she has now completed a foundation degree and is part way through a bachelor's degree, which will put her on course to make a career in medical research. This is a huge step from the rudderless, uncertain lady of five years previously. Her connection to the community and her reconnection with God has enabled her to be reconciled to herself. This is surely an aspect of atonement, as Christ is undoing the work of the fall, which damaged human relationships in four directions: with God, with others, with creation and with the self.

* * *

It is clear that through the ministries of Berrywood, God was engaging with the world. The examples shared above demonstrate aspects of his atoning action through Christ in the life of people in the St Crispin's community. Often when evaluating the success or viability of something, we intuitively head towards statistics or facts, things that can be verifiable. Hence the focus tends to be on numbers: attendees, baptisms, leaders and financial status. Other approaches like to focus on structure and practices. There is a degree to which we need to know these things, but they do not tell the whole story of a new ecclesial community – far from it. Since God is in the business of relationship, we also do well to pay attention to the stories of how he is at work in people's lives, drawing people to him, transforming them,

reconciling them, justifying them. Many of these stories will necessarily be anecdotal, although focused empirical research will
surely unearth deep and rich data, giving a fuller picture.

This cross-shaped approach to pioneering and fresh expressions of church allows us to cut through the debates about what
is or is not 'proper' church to focus on what God is actually
doing. God is active in all kinds of ways through pioneering
ministries and ecclesial initiatives that may look nothing like
the traditional church in the local area. We and many others
have seen people who may never have crossed the threshold of
a traditional church come to experience God's love and purpose for them. Through Christ they were being atoned, and
were able to experience this atonement through the work of the
fresh expression. As Christ died and rose again for all people,
who are we to limit what cultural expressions of mission and
worship are valid? Therefore if we need to ask evaluative questions of pioneering initiatives, the questions must concern how
the church is participating in God's action. Is this new ecclesial
community doing the work of church, by participating in God's
atoning action? Is the fresh expression of church providing and
creating spaces for God to be experienced and recognized? Are
they enabling people to reach out to God from their points of
nothingness, weakness and human limitation? Churchgoing in
traditional congregations remains in decline. It is time not only
for fresh expressions but also for the traditional church to be
judged by this cross-shaped criterion. If there is no experience
of atonement in some sense, perhaps the Church is not living up
to her calling. If there is no space for God to act or for people to
reach out to him, maybe a group does not deserve to have the
name 'church', regardless of what happens on a Sunday. When
we start from the point of God's engagement, we ensure that
the church remains cross-shaped and Jesus-focused.

Is it time to leave?

It's fair to say that we were not expecting to leave St Crispin's
after only five years. When I arrived I had expected it to take
between eight and ten years to develop the church to a point at

which it could continue. So it was a great surprise when we felt God calling loud and clear for us to move to a new role in the North East. We were not looking to move, I was not looking at job advertisements, so when the opportunity was initially put to us, our first reaction was to say that it was not the right time to move. Obedient to God, with a heavy heart but also with excitement at the new opportunities ahead, we moved to Durham in October 2015, five years and three months after arriving.

In the 1960s the Catholic Missionary Vincent Donovan spent 15 years in Tanzania with the Masai people. Catholic missionaries had been present in that part of Africa for over a century and had focused on building mission stations, schools and hospitals. This had the effect of taking local people out of their context for education, or in ones and twos, with the result that Christianity had not been fully accepted and indigenized. Usually when they returned to their tribes, the faith did not stick. Donovan embarked on a fresh approach, deciding to visit each tribe over a long period with the sole purpose of explaining the gospel to them. He spent over a year with each one. With the permission of the chiefs, he addressed whole tribes en masse, teaching them on a weekly basis in a contextually appropriate way. He would regularly mine the local stories and cultural practices to find the right words and illustrations to ensure the message could be heard. Once he felt he had explained all he could, he gave each tribe the opportunity to respond, which they tended to do as a group. Most tribes responded positively to the gospel, only one or two rejecting the faith. He then moved on to the next Masai tribe to start the process again, leaving each to contextualize the patterns and structures of worship for their own tribe, revisiting only occasionally to celebrate mass or give some direction. For the most part, leaders came from within the tribe. Donovan did this for 15 years before returning to the United States, never to return to Tanzania.

After spending such time with a people-group over so many years, you would expect Donovan to be fully invested in that place, reluctant to leave. However, he recognized the importance of leaving, allowing the Masai church to be fully owned by themselves: 'The final missionary step as regards any nation or culture, and the most important lesson we will ever teach them, is to leave them' (1982, p. 163). After all the work is done, the pioneer must move on to allow the gospel to be fully contextualized in the culture. Succession needs to be planned, and local leadership must emerge. According to George Lings, 'the characteristic of pioneers is that they are first in and also first out' (2011b, p. 35). As we were not expecting to leave, we had not put as much thought into leadership succession as we would have liked, and our announcement came as a shock. But in our last three months the core team pulled together and a presence was maintained in the community until a new leader could be appointed.

***

We had left a small community who were worshipping together, committed to reaching out to the wider community and eager to keep growing in faith. Through the practices of the church we had made regular contact with well over a hundred people, who either came to our groups or with whom we worked in the community. These relationships could be deepened and extended by the church community. The housing developers were just breaking ground on the new community centre, which would open up new possibilities for outreach in the St Crispin's development. Berrywood Church was ready for its next chapter, having recently joined a newly formed team of three Anglican churches in the parish of Duston, now under new leadership from a Team Rector with a missional heart. A new Team Vicar was to be appointed in my place to oversee Berrywood Church and take our pioneering initiative to the next stage. As we left, we hoped congregations and leadership alike would be able to see the mutual benefit of working together in a mixed economy of attractional and fresh expression of church. Leaving was difficult, but as we felt called by God to a new role in our ministries, we were confident to leave Berrywood in his hands.

Notes

1 Another report into five HTB-inspired church plants in East London revealed that in these churches, roughly 20 per cent of attendees were not previously attending any church when they joined (Thorlby, 2016, p. iii). This compares to 63 per cent of people who were not previously attending church, according to Church Army research into fresh expressions of all sizes in six dioceses (Dalpra and Vivian, 2016, p. 28).

2 George Lings, speaking at the Church Army Fresh Expression Research Conference, Sheffield, 4 Nov. 2016.

Bibliography

Albrecht, Daniel E., 'Pentecostal Spirituality: Looking Through the Lens of Ritual', *Pneuma* 14:2 (1996), pp. 107–25.

Anderson, Allan Heaton, *Introduction to Global Pentecostalism: Global Charismatic Christianity* (Cambridge: Cambridge University Press, 2004).

Archbishops' Council, Research and Statistics Department, *Celebrating Diversity in the Church of England: National Parish Congregation Diversity Monitoring* (2007): www.churchofengland.org/media/39089/gsmisc938.pdf; accessed 21 Sept. 2017.

Atkins, Martyn, *Resourcing Renewal: Shaping Churches for the Emerging Future* (Peterborough: Inspire, 2007).

Atkins, Martyn, 'What is the Essence of the Church?', in *Mission-Shaped Questions: Defining Issues for Today's Church*, ed. Steven Croft (London: Church House Publishing, 2008), pp. 16–28.

Aulén, Gustav, *Christus Victor* (London: SPCK, 1931).

Baker, Jonny, 'Prophetic Dialogue and Contemporary Culture', in *Mission on the Road to Emmaus: Constants, Context, and Prophetic Dialogue*, ed. Cathy Ross and Stephen B. Bevans (Maryknoll, NY: Orbis, 2015), pp. 201–14.

Barth, Karl, *Church Dogmatics*, 4 vols (London: T&T Clark, 2009).

Bauckham, Richard, 'The First Pioneers: Learning from the Acts of the Apostles', in *Pioneers 4 Life: Explorations in Theology and Wisdom for Pioneering Leaders*, ed. David Male (Abingdon: Bible Reading Fellowship, 2011), pp. 196–210.

Bauman, Zygmunt, *Liquid Modernity* (Cambridge: Polity Press, 2000).

Bede, *Commentary on Revelation*, trans. with intro. and notes by Faith Wallis (Liverpool: Liverpool University Press, 2013).

Beilby, James K. and Paul R. Eddy (eds), *The Nature of the Atonement: Four Views* (Downers Grove, IL: InterVarsity Press, 2006).

Bernardini, Jacopo, 'The Infantilization of the Postmodern Adult and the Figure of Kidult', *Postmodern Openings* 5:2 (2014), pp. 39–55.

Boff, Leonardo, *Ecclesiogenesis: The Base Communities Reinvent the Church* (London: Collins, 1986).

Boff, Leonardo, *Holy Trinity, Perfect Community* (Maryknoll, NY: Orbis, 2000).

Bordoni, Carlo, *Interregnum: Beyond Liquid Modernity* (Bielefeld: transcript Verlag, 2016).

Boyd, Gregory A., 'Christus Victor View', in *The Nature of the Atonement: Four Views*, ed. James Beilby and Paul R. Eddy (Downers Grove, IL: InterVarsity Press, 2006), pp. 24–49.

Breen, Mike and Walt Kallestad, *The Passionate Church: The Art of Life-Changing Discipleship* (Colorado Springs, CO: NexGen, 2005).

Brierley, Peter (ed.), *British Religion in the 21st Century: What the Statistics Indicate* (Religious Trends, no. 7) (Swindon: Christian Research, 2008).

Bruce, Steve, *God is Dead: Secularization in the West* (Oxford: Blackwell, 2002).

Church of England, Mission and Public Affairs Council, *Mission-Shaped Church: Church Planting and Fresh Expressions of Church in a Changing Context* (London: Church House Publishing, 2004).

Cray, Graham, 'Communities of the Kingdom', in *Fresh Expressions of Church and the Kingdom of God*, ed. Graham Cray, Aaron Kennedy and Ian Mobsby (Norwich: Canterbury Press, 2012), pp. 13–28.

Croft, Steven, 'Fresh Expressions in a Mixed Economy Church: A Perspective', in *Mission-Shaped Questions: Defining Issues for Today's Church*, ed. Steven Croft (London: Church House Publishing, 2008a), pp. 1–15.

Croft, Steven, 'Mapping Ecclesiology for a Mixed Economy', in *Mission-Shaped Questions: Defining Issues for Today's Church*, ed. Steven Croft (London: Church House Publishing, 2008b), pp. 188–9.

Dalpra, Claire, 'When is Messy Church 'church'?', in *Messy Church Theology: Exploring the Significance of Messy Church for the Wider Church*, ed. George Lings (Abingdon: Bible Reading Fellowship, 2013), pp. 12–30.

Dalpra, Claire and John Vivian, *Who's There?: The Church Backgrounds of Attenders in Anglican Fresh Expressions of Church* (Sheffield: Church Army Research Unit, 2016).

Davie, Grace, *Religion in Britain: A Persistent Paradox* (Chichester: Wiley Blackwell, 2015).

Davison, Andrew and Alison Milbank, *For the Parish: A Critique of Fresh Expressions* (London, SCM Press, 2010).

Donovan, Vincent, *Christianity Rediscovered* (London: SCM Press, 1982).

Drane, John, *After McDonaldization: Mission, Ministry, and Christian Discipleship in an Age of Uncertainty* (London: Darton, Longman & Todd, 2008).

Driver, John, *Understanding the Atonement for the Mission of the Church* (Scottdale, PA: Herald Press, 1986).

Dulles, Avery, *Models of the Church: A Critical Assessment of the Church in all its Aspects* (Dublin: Gill & Macmillan, 1974).

Dunlop, Andrew, 'Five Year Update!', *Diary of a Pioneer Minister* (Personal Blog, 18 June 2015): https://pioneerminister.wordpress.com/2015/06/18/five-year-update; accessed 21 Aug. 2017.

Dutton, Christine, 'Unpicking Knit and Natter', *Ecclesial Practices* 1:1 (2014), pp. 31–50.

Fahey, Michael, 'Church', in *Systematic Theology: Roman Catholic Perspectives, Vol. 2*, ed. Francis Schüssler Fiorenza and John P. Galvin (Minneapolis, MN: Fortress Press, 1992), pp. 1–74.

Fiddes, Paul, *Participating in God: A Pastoral Doctrine of the Trinity* (London: Darton, Longman & Todd, 2000).

Flett, John, *The Witness of God* (Grand Rapids, MI: Eerdmans, 2010).

Francis, Leslie and Philip Richter, *Gone for Good: Church-Leaving and Returning in the 21st Century* (Peterborough: Epworth Press, 2007).

Fresh Expressions in the Mission of the Church: Report of an Anglican–Methodist Working Party (London: Church House Publishing, 2012).

Girard, René, *I See Satan Fall Like Lightning* (Maryknoll, NY: Orbis, 2001).

Goodhew, David (ed.), *Church Growth in Britain: 1980 to the Present* (Farnham: Ashgate, 2012).

Goodhew, David, 'An Introduction', in *Towards a Theology of Church Growth*, ed. David Goodhew (Farnham: Ashgate, 2015a).

Goodhew, David and Rob Barward-Symmons, *New Churches in the North East* (Durham: Centre for Church Growth Research, 2015b).

Goodhew, David (ed.), *Growth and Decline in the Anglican Communion: 1980 to the Present* (London: Routledge, 2017).

Gorman, Michael, 'Effecting the New Covenant: A (Not So) New, New Testament Model for the Atonement', *Ex Auditu* 26 (2010), pp. 26–59.

Green, Joel B. and Mark D. Baker, *Recovering the Scandal of the Cross: Atonement in New Testament and Contemporary Contexts* (Downers Grove, IL: InterVarsity Press, 2000).

Gregory, Brian 'A Cruciform Mission? Missional Embodiment of the Atonement', *Wesleyan Theological Journal* 50:1 (2015), p. 157.

Gutiérrez, Gustavo, *A Theology of Liberation: History, Politics, and Salvation*, rev. edn (London: SCM Press, 1988 [1974]).

Hedley, Freddy, *Lessons from Antioch: Exploring a Biblical Guide for the Contemporary Church* (Swaffham: Emblem, 2010).

Hiebert, Paul G., *Anthropological Insights for Missionaries* (Grand Rapids, MI: Baker Books, 1985).

Hollinghurst, Steve, 'When is Messy Church 'not church'?', in *Messy Church Theology: Exploring the Significance of Messy Church for the Wider Church*, ed. George Lings (Abingdon: Bible Reading Fellowship, 2013), pp. 31–47.

Holmes, Stephen, 'Trinitarian Missiology: Towards a Theology of God as Missionary', *International Journal of Systematic Theology* 8:1 (2006), pp. 72–90.

Holmes, Stephen, 'Three Versus One? Some Problems of Social Trinitarianism', *Journal of Reformed Theology* 3:1 (2009), pp. 77–89.

Holmes, Stephen, *The Quest for the Trinity: The Doctrine of God in Scripture, History and Modernity* (Downers Grove, IL: InterVarsity Press, 2012).

Hull, John, *Mission-Shaped Church: A Theological Response* (London: SCM Press, 2006).

Jewett, Robert, *Romans: A Commentary* (Minneapolis, MI: Fortress Press, 2007).

Jüngel, Eberhard, 'The World as Possibility and Actuality: The Ontology of the Doctrine of Justification', in Eberhard Jüngel, *Theological Essays*, trans. J. B. Webster (London: T&T Clark, 1989), pp. 95–123.

Jüngel, Eberhard, *Justification: The Heart of the Christian Faith*, trans. Jeffrey F. Cayzer, (Edinburgh: T&T Clark, 2001).

Kilby, Karen, 'Perichoresis and Projection', *New Blackfriars* 81:957 (2000), pp. 432–45.

Kim, Kirsteen, 'Mission Theology of the Church', *International Review of Mission* 99:1 (2010), pp. 39–55.

Lings, George, *New Town, New Church: Deep Excavations* (Encounters on the Edge, no. 52) (Sheffield: Church Army, 2011a).

Lings, George, 'Looking in the Mirror: What makes a Pioneer?', in *Pioneers 4 Life: Explorations in Theology and Wisdom for Pioneering Leaders*, ed. David Male (Abingdon: Bible Reading Fellowship, 2011b), pp. 30–47.

Lings, George 'A History of Fresh Expressions and Church Planting in the Church of England', in *Church Growth in Britain: 1980 to the Present*, ed. David Goodhew (Farnham: Ashgate, 2012), pp. 161–78.

Lings, George, *The Day of Small Things: An Analysis of Fresh Expressions of Church in 21 Dioceses* (Sheffield: Church Army Research Centre, 2016).

Lings, George, *Reproducing Churches* (Abingdon: BRF, 2017).

Luther, Martin, *Augsburg Confession* (Milwaukee, WI: Northwestern Publishing House, 2005): www.stpls.com/uploads/4/4/8/0/44802893/augsburg-confession.pdf; accessed 8 Sept. 2017.

MaGee, Greg, 'The Origins of the Church at Rome' (2008): https://bible.org/article/origins-church-rome; accessed 28 June 2017.

Male, Dave, *Church Unplugged: Remodelling Church without Losing your Soul* (Milton Keynes: Authentic, 2008).

Male, David, *How to Pioneer (Even if You Haven't a Clue)* (London: Church House Publishing, 2016).

Mann, Alan, *Atonement for a 'Sinless' Society: Engaging with an Emerging Culture* (Milton Keynes: Paternoster, 2005).

McGavran, Donald A., *Bridges of God: A Study in the Strategy of Missions* (London: World Dominion Press, 1955).

McKnight, Scot, *A Community Called Atonement* (Nashville, TN: Abingdon, 2007), pp. 107–14.

Milbank, John, 'Stale Expressions: The Management-Shaped Church', *Studies in Christian Ethics* 21:1 (2008), pp. 117–28.

Mobsby, Ian, *Emerging and Fresh Expressions of Church* (London: Moot Community Publishing, 2007).

Mobsby, Ian, *The Becoming of G-d* (Cambridge: YTC Press, 2008).

Mobsby, Ian J., *God Unknown: The Trinity in Contemporary Spirituality* (Norwich: Canterbury Press, 2012).

Moltmann, Jürgen, *The Way of Jesus Christ: Christology in Messianic Dimensions* (San Francisco, CA: HarperSanFrancisco, 1990).

Moore, Paul, *Making Discipleship in Messy Church: Growing Faith in an All-Age Community* (Abingdon: Bible Reading Fellowship, 2013).

Moynagh, Michael with Philip Harrold, *Church for Every Context: An Introduction to Theology and Practice* (London: SCM Press, 2012).

Moynagh, Michael, *Being Church, Doing Life: Creating Gospel Communities where Life Happens* (Oxford: Monarch, 2014).

Moynagh, Michael, *Church in Life: Innovation, Mission and Ecclesiology* (London: SCM Press, 2017).

Murray, Stuart, *Church Planting: Laying Foundations* (Carlisle: Paternoster, 1998), p. 31.

Neill, Stephen, *The Unfinished Task* (London: Edinburgh House Press, 1957).

Nouwen, Henri, *The Selfless Way of Christ: Downward Mobility and the Spiritual Life* (London: Darton, Longman & Todd, 2007).

Percy, Martyn, 'Old Tricks for New Dogs? A critique of Fresh Expressions', in *Evaluating Fresh Expressions: Explorations in Emerging Church*, ed. Louise Nelstrop and Martyn Percy (Norwich: Canterbury Press, 2008), pp. 27–39.

Pugh, Ben, *Atonement Theories: A Way Through the Maze* (Eugene, OR: Cascade, 2014).

Richebächer, Wilhelm, 'Missio Dei: The Basis of Mission Theology or a Wrong Path?', *International Review of Mission* 92:367 (2003), pp. 588–605.

Riddell, Mike, 'Bread and Wine, Beer and Pies', in *Mass Culture: Eucharist and Mission in a Post-Modern World*, ed. Pete Ward (Oxford: Bible Reading Fellowship, 1999), pp. 95–115.

Root, Andrew, *Christopraxis: A Practical Theology of the Cross* (Minneapolis, MN: Fortress Press, 2014).

Sankey, Jenny, 'With, Through and In Christ: A Eucharistic Approach to Atonement', in *Atonement Today: A Symposium at St John's College, Nottingham*, ed. John Goldingay (London: SPCK, 1995), pp. 93–110.

Schmiechen, Peter, *Saving Power: Theories of Atonement and Forms of the Church* (Grand Rapids, MI: Eerdmans, 2005).

Schmiechen, Peter, *Defining the Church for Our Time: Origin and Structure, Variety and Viability* (Eugene OR: Cascade, 2012).

Shier-Jones, Angela, *Pioneer Ministry and Fresh Expressions of Church* (London: SPCK, 2009).

Thorlby, Tim, *Love, Sweat and Tears: Church Planting in East London* (London: Centre of Theology and Community, 2016).

Thumma, Scott and Dave Travis, *Beyond Megachurch Myths: What We Can Learn from America's Largest Churches* (San Francisco, CA: Wiley, 2007).

van den Toren, Benno, 'Can We See the Naked Theological Truth', in Matthew Cook, Rob Haskell, Ruth Julian and Natee Tanchanpongs (eds), *Local Theology for the Global Church: Principles for an Evangelical Approach to Contextualization* (Pasadena, CA: William Carey, 2010), pp. 91–108.

Volland, Michael, *Through the Pilgrim Door: Pioneering a Fresh Expression of Church* (Eastbourne: Survivor, 2009).

von Balthasar, Hans Urs, *Theo-Drama (Vol. IV): The Action* (San Francisco: Ignatius Press, 1994).

Walton, Roger, 'Have we got the Missio Dei right?', *Epworth Review* 35:3 (2008), pp. 42–3.

Ward, Pete, *Liquid Church* (Milton Keynes: Paternoster, 2002).

Warren, Robert, *Being Human, Being Church: Spirituality and Mission in the Local Church* (London: Marshall Pickering, 1995).

Wier, Andy, *Who's There: The Church Backgrounds of Attenders in Anglican Fresh Expressions of Church* (Sheffield: Church Army, 2016): www.churcharmy.org/Publisher/File.aspx?ID=180861; accessed 7 July 2017.

Williams, Rowan, 'Transcript of Keynote Address by Archbishop of Canterbury, 23rd June 2004': www.acpi.org.uk/articles/archbishops%20address.htm; accessed 23 June 2016.

Withington, Brian, 'Evaluating Pioneer Ministry: Use of Milestones', *Resourcing Mission Bulletin* (Church Growth Research and Development, October 2011): www.churchgrowthrd.org.uk/UserFiles/File/Resourcing_Mission_Bulletin/Oct_2011/Evaluating_Pioneer_Ministry_October_2011.pdf; accessed 2 July 2016.

Zizioulas, John, *Being as Communion: Studies in Personhood* (London: Darton, Longman & Todd, 1985).

Index of Names and Subjects